W9-CQN-884

THE STRICKEN LUTE

THE STRICKEN LUTE

An Account of the Life of Peter Abelard

BY

ROGER B. LLOYD

Peace, O my stricken lute!
Thy strings are sleeping.
Would that my heart could still
Its bitter weeping!

ABELARD.

The Lament of David for Jonathan.

KENNIKAT PRESS
Port Washington, N. Y./London

THE STRICKEN LUTE

First published in 1932
Reissued in 1971 by Kennikat Press
Library of Congress Catalog Card No: 73-118535
ISBN 0-8046-1158-0

Manufactured by Taylor Publishing Company   Dallas, Texas

TO MY WIFE

NON ENIM MECUM ANIMUS MEUS
SED TECUM HABITAVIT. SED ET
NUNC MAXIME SI TECUM NON EST
NUSQUAM EST. ESSE VERO SINE TE
NEQUAQUAM POTEST.

HELOISE, *Letters.*

PREFACE

It is an author's pleasant duty, when he finishes his book, to make acknowledgment of his obligations. First and foremost, then, I am indebted, as every biographer of Abelard must be, to the standard book on the subject, Charles de Rémusat's *Abélard*, published in Paris in 1845. Although it is true that a good deal of knowledge of Abelard and his times has been made available since 1845, de Rémusat's book is not likely to be superseded. He is the pioneer; and to him all modern students of Abelard's life must pay homage. I also owe a great deal to a very different work, Mr George Moore's *Heloise and Abelard*, for it was my enthralment over that beautiful novel which first stirred my curiosity about Abelard, and tempted me to write this biography. As in private duty bound, I must make grateful mention of two other names, the late Professor R. Lane Poole, of whose work no student of the twelfth century in general, and of contemporary scholasticism in particular, can afford to be ignorant; and also Miss Helen Waddell, to whose charming books, *The Wandering Scholars* and *Mediæval Latin Lyrics*, I owe a debt which can hardly be adequately discharged. I am further indebted to her for her ready permission to allow me to quote her fine translations of Abelard's poems.

I have acknowledged the sources of all quotations in the footnotes, except those taken from the *Letters* themselves. Every quotation from them is taken from Scott-Moncrieff's translation, published by Guy Chapman in 1925. Though I have ventured to dissent from various statements he makes in his preface, my debt to his work is plainly heavy, since the greater part of any biography of Abelard must naturally be based on his own account of his life as written by him in the first of the *Letters, Historia Calamitatum.*

After some hesitation I have adopted the well-known spelling of the names Abelard and Heloise, even though *Abailard* and *Heloissa* may be more historically accurate.

R. B. L.

May 1932.

THE STRICKEN LUTE

I

IN the year when Abelard was born, 1079, the curtain was slowly rising upon the most vivid, and, in a sense, the most satisfactory century of Christian history. The Golden Middle Age was at hand, which was to redeem mediævalism from the slurs cast upon it by the dark centuries of the barbarian invasions and by the chaotic intrigues and wars of the Carolingian monarchs. That age comprised the first, and perhaps the greater Renaissance. But it did not achieve its greatest glory until more than a hundred and fifty years had passed, until St Thomas Aquinas had laboured to give a final and considered expression of the intellectual ground the Golden Middle Age had won. Its earlier phase, in which the world was made safe for the new thinking, coincides with, and is itself the career of Peter Abelard and his immediate disciples.

In 1079 the earlier mediæval spirit, the spirit of the great abbots, austere, heroic, tough, and obscurantist, was in full command. It had been challenged, but only by a few lone voices crying in the wilderness, and they had had little effect. Thus, the first task of this Renaissance was the replacement of the old spirit by the new. That inevitably meant conflict, and Abelard was the man upon whom the brunt of that conflict fell. It broke him; but from the ashes of his final humiliation the new fire was kindled. It blazed until a new Europe had risen from its flames. The twelfth century is to the thirteenth as the spirit of youth is to the staider, the more serene wisdom of middle age. The difference between them is the difference between Abelard and Aquinas.

It would be difficult to mention any form of mediæval activity into which the twelfth century did not breathe a new creative effort. In that century architecture broke its old bonds and created new forms. Romanesque art achieved the highest pitch of perfection of which it was capable; and it was promptly superseded by Gothic. The great Gothic cathedrals were most of them begun or finished within the century's limits; and to those years belong Canterbury, Noyon, Laon, and, perhaps greatest of all, Chartres. Sculpture, handicrafts, handwriting all changed their forms, became graceful where they had been stiff, and took on a new lease of life. The art of war was extended and revolutionised by the first three Crusades of 1096, 1147, and 1189. The old monastic fervour, which seemed to have halted a hundred years before with the foundation of Cluny, suddenly blazed forth again in the establishment of the two purest of the mediæval orders, the Cistercians and the Carthusians. Nor was the century content with superabundant making of history; it fathered a new and an ampler technique in its writing of history. Memoirs and biographies, universal histories and local chronicles, codified annals of courts and monasteries were written everywhere both in Latin and in the Vernacular, and present an *embarras de richesses* to the modern historian. In the more purely creative activities of literature there was an equal profusion of writing, ranging from the establishment of the new liturgical drama to the mingled beauty and scurrility of the Goliardic songbooks. At the apex of all these forms of creative expression the Papacy sat enthroned, and that too passed in the twelfth century from weakness to strength until, with the enthronement of Innocent III in 1198, it came to the fullest flowering of its power.

Yet there is a sense in which it is true to say that none of these departments of activity held the keys of the future. Through none of them was mediævalism destined to make its characteristic contribution to civilisation. One may, perhaps, make an exception in the case of Gothic architecture, for the great cathedrals are still in daily use, still nourish the souls of thousands of Christian people, and are still powerful as architectural influences. But the success of Innocent III was such that it indirectly involved the Papacy in the sixteenth-century revolution against its power. We no longer write our history in the style of the chroniclers. The movement for vernacular literature was evanescent, and three centuries later Roger Ascham could be solemnly reproved for his barbarous innovation in writing in his native tongue. Strip the Crusades of their superficially epic and romantic

trappings and they are little more than crude and
minor forays, with little effect upon the course of
history.

None of these constitutes the characteristically
mediæval contribution to civilisation. Yet that contribution was the gift of the twelfth century, and it
was the university.

Universities, of course, were not precisely founded.
They were evolved by an easy and natural extension of
the more elastic of the two earlier educational institutions, the cathedral schools. By the twelfth century
the cathedral schools, established in cities under direct
episcopal and diocesan control, had completely wrested
from the old monastic schools their previous reputation
of being the foremost centres of learning. They were
combinations of the modern county grammar school
and diocesan theological college; and they furnished
by far the best education that Europe then had to give.
Ambitious boys must study there, and obtain the hall-
mark of a Chartres or a Paris education, or must give
up their ambitions. These schools were to be found
in most parts of Europe, but it was in Northern France
that they were strongest and most numerous; and it
was therefore Northern France that became the centre
of gravity of the university movement in its early
years, and the battleground of the warfare between the
old and the new theology.

The outward condition which distinguishes a
mediæval university from the cathedral school, which
was its parent, is the intricacy of its mechanism. When
you find a company of boys and young men studying

together under a master, unhampered and undirected by very much organisation, as at Chartres, that is a cathedral school. But when you find an ample and intricate organisation, a recognition of exclusive privileges, guilds for masters, *nationes* and proctors for students, you have a university. The one grew out of the other, and the achievement of the twelfth century in this field lies in providing the impetus which made that growth possible.

That impetus lay in an impalpable quickening of the intellect. A book on the causes of that quickening still awaits an author, and in its absence it almost seems as though the twelfth-century Renaissance came to its birth in a night, as though men woke up one morning,

    "Look'd at each other with a wild surmise—
    Silent——"

In 1100 the very air of Western Europe was quick with philosophic surmise. From cottages as far apart as Scotland and Sicily there came young men setting forth on the long and exhausting tramp to the school and the master of their choice. Learning had quite suddenly come to be valued as one of the most precious things in life, and in 1079, when Abelard was born, this intellectual revolution was just beginning to have its effect upon Europe as a whole.

But tendencies have to be expressed in terms of personality if ever they are to become popular; and it was because Chartres, greatest of all cathedral schools, was content to rely upon the excellence of its syllabus rather than upon the personal magnetism of its teachers that it never attracted sufficient students for it to become a university. This intellectual quickening was an atmosphere. It had to find a leader, who summed up in himself all for which it stood, before it could become a movement. That leader was Peter Abelard. In a very real sense he was the movement. His was the magnetism which attracted the mass of wandering scholars; and his destiny it was to fight the dialectician's battle against the older theology. To him, more than to any other man, we owe not only our universities, but also the legacy of the twelfth century to civilisation.

II

The people responsible for this great burst of creative activity were themselves exuberantly alive. That liveliness naturally took many forms. It varied from the reckless, cynical geniality of the Goliards to the single-minded austerity of the Cistercians. Arnold of Brescia and St Bernard himself were equally typical of their century in their several ways. But linking them to each other, and to all the other great men of the age, there was another quality besides the exuberance of their activity. That quality was a certain inner integrity, a singleness of purpose. They conceived their lives as possessing a quite definite purpose and end; and, for the most part, they pursued it through thick and thin.

Turning to the actors in the smaller drama that was

Abelard's life, it is thus possible to label them. St Bernard is the saintly fanatic, whose saintliness is not in the least denied by his fanaticism. His only enemies are those he conceives to be his Church's enemies: against them he is adamant, but his love flows over the rest of the world. William of Champeau is the teacher past his prime who cannot bring himself to quit the scene of his triumphs, and whose supreme failing is jealousy. Arnold of Brescia is the fanatic disciple on the other side of the controversy. John Roscelin is the scholar soured and embittered by misfortune. Even for Heloise it is possible to discover a formula which applies to all her motives—the integrity of unfailing constancy.

The actors can all be docketed. Their singleness of purpose is such that in varying situations their motives are always clear, and their reaction to the challenges of their changing circumstances becomes almost mechanical. Yet they are never dead and never dull; and they are very seldom ineffective. The malleability which the historian finds in them is no sign of tameness, for there is no set of characters more vividly and more exuberantly alive. Heloise, Bernard, Arnold of Brescia, William of Champeau, John Roscelin—they all had life and had it abundantly.

Abelard himself was not less vital than they, but he is less easily understood. No formula covers his motives or explains his nature. He was a churchman, but more than that. He was a teacher, one of the greatest the world has known, but he was continually turning away from his pupils. He was a lover, and in that guise nearly inexplicable. He was a philosopher, a theologian, a poet, all these by turns and none of them for very long at a time. His impulses were genuinely religious and genuinely sensual. He was sincerely resigned to authority and at the same time viewed his revolt as a vocation. He was morbid and introspective, and yet enjoyed the clearest vision of all events not directly affecting himself. He perpetually dramatised himself, but there was in him none of the weakness which that habit so frequently involves.

It follows that there is always a difficulty in understanding his motives, and that his own words cannot be accepted as evidence for these motives without caution. His capacity for emotional experience was tremendous. His imagination was always taut and quivering. There was no fact in his experience of life out of which he did not extract the last drop of emotion; and yet his vitality was such that no matter what demands were made upon them, his emotional reserves were never drained. Such a nature lives in the moment. For him a momentary experience was so absorbing, and he lived it with such complete abandon, that he lacked any real sense of proportion. He could never correct the present depression by reflecting on past joy. If his circumstances were joyful, he gave himself body and soul to realising and savouring that joy. If they were sad and gloomy, as when he wrote *Historia Calamitatum*, he must soak himself in their gloom, see himself as wholly abandoned to despair, and every detail of his career as contributing to that despair. Such a man will live intensely, and may make a mark upon history—but he will never write good autobiography. This is important because the main authority for the facts of Abelard's life is his own account of them, *Historia Calamitatum*, which was written during his blackest period, and in consequence is a gloomy, morbid document. Like most pieces of morbidity it is a flagrant distortion not of historic facts but of the subtleties of character, and if it is taken at its face value it is apt to lead the student astray. Scott-Moncrieff, for example, whose perception was certainly acute, and to whom we owe the only authoritative and definitive translation of the *Letters* into English, has been thus led astray. In his preface he permits himself to write of Abelard as an "intolerable old egoist" and an "irrepressible young prig."

Epithets such as Scott-Moncrieff's, as a final appraisement of Abelard's character, are plainly absurd. Intolerable old egoists and irrepressible young prigs do not make the stir in history that Abelard did. Yet that is very much the picture which emerges from the gloomy pages of the *Historia Calamitatum*, and which Abelard therefore drew of himself. His habits of self-dramatisation have led others besides himself astray. The *Historia Calamitatum* has to be treated with caution when used as anything more than evidence for the bare historic facts, for we are bound to recognise that his most vital characteristic was charm. The contemporary records hide his charm, but the young loved to be with him. They flocked to him in adversity as in prosperity, and they never forgot him when they were old. Miss Helen Waddell's fine reverence in her delightful *Wandering Scholars* may be excessive, but it is nearer the truth than Scott-Moncrieff's disdain. Writing of some obscure clerk, she quotes the famous line,

"And did you once see Shelley plain?"

and comments—"Shelley? This man may have spoken to Peter Abelard!"[1]

His life is like the overture of a Wagner opera, compounded of motifs. As the years unfold, these motifs dominate them, each in turn. There is the Heloise motif, the scholar motif; and the other interests which made the unity of his life are all perfectly recognisable when they are heard—the abbot, the theologian, the victim of persecution. One by one these themes are heard. One by one they dominate the piece, until at last, as in an overture, they merge together in a closing motif, which is peace.

III

Abelard was fortunate in his father. His name was Berenger, and he was a minor Breton nobleman of Palais, about eight miles from Nantes, between that town and Poitiers. The *Historia Calamitatum* begins with a sketch of Berenger. It is a slight but sufficient portrait of a man bound to a profession he found unattractive, whose work lay in such matters as going

[1] Helen Waddell, *The Wandering Scholars*, p. 146. (Constable.)

to the wars and administering an estate, while his
heart yearned for scholarship. But the pursuit of
letters in that age was the vocation of a lifetime rather
than the pastime of a dilettante. Fate had given
Berenger an aptitude for letters, and then buckled
him into a soldier's gear. He had to be content to
know enough to realise that the great prizes of learning
must for ever remain outside his reach. His was a
scholar's mind imprisoned in the body of a minor
nobleman, bound by feudal ties to the exacting behest
of the Dukes of Brittany.

Such a personality, baulked of his own secret ambitions, is apt to dream his visions over again in and
for his son. Such a one, in a later age, was the
delightful father of Robert Browning, poet at heart but
inexorably a banker by profession. So it was with
Berenger. Genius could ask for no better father.
In his eldest son, Peter Abelard, the signs of any
aptitude for scholarship were eagerly sought, gladly
recognised, and warmly encouraged. It is not surprising that when the boy announced that he proposed
to resign his seignorial rights to his younger brother,
and to take to the life of a peripatetic—a wandering
scholar, he was commended by his father, and his
mother, Lucy.

It was in dialectic, which, in a limited sense, is the
art of logical argument, that the boy chiefly excelled.
One method of pursuing the art was to set out on
foot, and to wander about France from school to
school and teacher to teacher, seeking fellow travellers
by the way on whom to sharpen the wits. It was the

old method of Socrates and Plato—the encounter, the pleasant walk in shady lanes, and the long exhilarating talk on high matters of philosophy. He was perhaps sixteen or seventeen years old when he set out to emulate the Peripatetics, and to become one of the knight-errants of philosophy. He went from province to province, seeking new teachers and worthy opponents for his extraordinarily keen wits, and learning from each controversy more and more of the art of dialectics, and becoming increasingly proficient in metaphysical technique.

In the last decade of the eleventh century one great problem of metaphysics formed the staple of scholarly conversation—the Nominalist and Realist controversy. And wherever men were gathered together over a discussion of the controversy, the name of one who had scorched himself in its flames very soon crept into the talk.

The name was John Roscelin. He was a monk from Compiègne, a subtle and experienced dialectician, who had ventured to beard such pillars of orthodoxy as Lanfranc and Peter Damian, by raising again the dust of the old insoluble problem of the nature of Universals. He had publicly identified himself with the extreme nominalist position. In a reckless, but, for himself, an unfortunate moment he had applied his Nominalism to the doctrine of the Trinity. To demonstrate the absurdity of Realism as it was taught in the orthodox schools, he proclaimed that if reality lies in the universal, then the three Persons of the Trinity must be not three but one, and the Father and the Holy Spirit must be incarnate with and in the Son. That position he disavowed. But in seeking to ridicule the one heresy, he fell into a worse one himself, for he maintained that reality lay in the individual unit of the species. Applying this to the Trinity, he denied the unity of the Godhead by admitting the reality only of the three divine persons, and by saying that we should properly speak not of one God, but of three.

It was to proclaim tritheism, to divide the indivisible Trinity. In seeking to impale the realists on the one horn of his dilemma, he had only succeeded in impaling himself on the other and the sharper horn. The realists rushed to battle. Peter Damian vehemently protested against that or any other attempt to understand the divine mysteries. Anselm wrote *The Reality of Universals* in order to refute the heretic by using his own dialectical weapons. The Council of Soissons, sitting in 1092, condemned his teaching as false in itself and incompatible with the doctrine of the Holy Trinity. To be branded as a heretic in the Middle Ages was no laughing matter. Roscelin resigned the canonry of Compiègne which he held, and abruptly departed to England.

For a short time he stayed in England. Perhaps he took Anselm's polemic on the Reality of Universals with him, and read it during his enforced seclusion, for late in the next year, 1093, he got into touch with Anselm. He professed that he had been convinced of the error of his ways, and recanted, a little suddenly, his former errors and heresies. He was allowed to return to France, and was given a scholastic post at St Mary of Loches in Touraine, where he taught such scholars as resorted to him.

Among his pupils was Abelard. Whether he sought him out before the Council of Soissons, in England, or in Touraine is unknown. But probably it was before Roscelin went to Touraine, for the teaching of Roscelin's which Abelard spoke so contemptuously about was certainly nominalist in tendency, and he would be unlikely to be offending again in the very year after his condemnation.

In the *Historia Calamitatum* Abelard ignores the episode of his pupillage to Roscelin. He passes straight from his departure from home to his entry into William of Champeau's school at Paris, and says nothing about the four years of his wandering. Elsewhere, however, he says himself that he had Roscelin for a master, and, in a not over-courteous phrase, that he found his teaching "the vapourings of a lunatic." Roscelin retorted in kind by reminding Abelard in a letter that he had been the most insignificant of all his pupils. Roscelin was proud and fiery, and he had the scholars' vanity which is slower to forget imputations on his scholarship than upon his morals. Abelard had all his master's pride and instability of temper, and, at that time, uncommon pertinacity. Crudely and roughly he challenged his master's exposition, putting the famous and unanswerable question with which, by slightly changing the terms, he afterwards shattered William of Champeau. There was an explosion, and then the smouldering embers of a

quarrel which was never healed. Years afterwards
these embers were to flame again, and to scorch
Abelard by their heat. Roscelin was standing near to
his own humiliation. But it was his destiny to stand
forth later as a champion of orthodoxy, and to be
numbered among those who helped to procure his
pupil's condemnation by a Council which, by a curious
chance, was to be held in the very city which had been
the scene of his own humiliation. Abelard had made
his first enemy, and Roscelin was a dangerous enemy
to have made.

The chronology of Abelard's wandering is vague.
It is supposed by some authorities, notably Dr Lane
Poole, that he spent a year, between leaving Roscelin
and arriving at Paris, at the great school of Chartres,
where he vainly tried to grasp the rudiments of mathematics under the instruction of the mathematician
Tirric. Rémusat, on the other hand, in his *Vie
d'Abélard*, puts it some years later. The exact date,
however, is of small importance, for the Quadrivium,
except that part of it which was the study of music, was
hardly the kind of course to have much effect on his
essentially intuitive mind. Tirric taught him little;
and in later years he wrote, à propos of a certain
geometrical problem in Boethius: "As to its solution,
I have heard many propounded by mathematicians.
But I prefer not to judge between them, for I know
myself to be completely ignorant of that art."

IV

In 1100, when he was twenty-one, Abelard came to Paris, and sought admission to the school of Notre Dame, where William of Champeau was charming the ears of scholars from all over Western Europe.

As all roads once led to Rome, so in the Paris of the twelfth century all academic discussions led sooner or later to the problem of problems, the question of Nominalism and Realism. The controversy was concerned with the nature of universals, and their relation to individual things. Is "Humanity" a mere name given for the sake of convenience to denote the totality of human beings? Or is "Humanity" a real essence having an objective existence of its own? The realist, leaning on Plato, would say that "Humanity" was a real substance, identical in every man and woman, and would explain their manifest differences by postulating a mere fortuitous concourse of "accidents" to account for them. The nominalist denied that "Humanity" was any more than the name given to the general mass of men and women to distinguish them from the general mass of dogs or fish. Take the dogma of the Holy Trinity and apply this distinction to it, as Roscelin had done, and it at once becomes obvious that orthodoxy is always Realist, and that Nominalism must always be on the defensive, because by its nature it skates delicately on the thin ice of heresy.

This question was no new academic subtlety, propounded in the same spirit as the famous—and libellous—question of how many angels could dance on the point of a needle, or the other celebrated conundrum, especially in vogue at Bologna, nursery of archdeacons, as to whether it was possible that an archdeacon could be saved. It was, and it is, the problem of problems. Beginning in the realm of philosophy, it leads him who wrestles with it into physics, ethics, and theology, and, as Rashdall used to say, "he who suggests a solution has in fact propounded his theory of the universe."

Until after Abelard's death in 1142, the mediæval scholars possessed only fragments of the works of both Plato and Aristotle. Plato was represented by a Latin translation of a part of the *Timæus*, and Aristotle by his *Categories* and the *De Interpretatione*, both of them in Boethius' translation. Meagre remnants indeed! but it happens that in those fragments are contained both Plato's and Aristotle's doctrines of Universals. Thus it came about that this discussion, which arose in many forms, was the most vital controversy of the Middle Ages.

The whole atmosphere of the early Church had been Platonic, and in this respect Platonism was synonymous with orthodoxy. Before the discovery of Aristotle's *Organon*, Plato was universally considered to be the greatest of all philosophers. It was true that less was directly known of his work than of Aristotle's, but his champions were so much more influential. St Augustine, for instance, never forgot the neo-Platonism which had rescued him from his gloomy Manicheean beliefs, and had brought him to Christ. No man towered more portentously over the mediæval Church or had a comparable influence on mediæval scholarship than he. Porphyry, whose *Isagoge* was a work known and quoted by every mediæval thinker, Abelard among them, was himself an ardent Platonist. So was Boethius, to whom the Middle Ages were indebted for his translations of Aristotle, and his *Consolation of Philosphy*. Macrobius, whose influence on the Middle Ages was only less than that of Augustine, Porphyry, and Boethius, and whose gloss of Plotinus could be found in every library, was also an enthusiastic Platonist. He had spoken of Plato as the greatest of all philosophers. But Aristotle was known only as a dialectician, only by such of his works as had then been translated. Plato's fame was far less limited. Little of what he wrote was then available, but he was known to have scaled all heights. The mediæval attitude to the two sages is aptly typified by a distinction drawn by Cassiodorus, who spoke of Aristotle as "The Logician," but of Plato— paying the greatest reverence he knew—as "Plato the Theologian."

Thus, so far as this controversy is concerned, Platonism is synonymous with orthodoxy. In another important connection Plato was regarded as fathering heresies, as Abelard was to discover. But for the purposes of Nominalism and Realism, Plato was invoked as the "onlie begetter" of extreme Realism, and the Aristotelian logic was suspect.

The whole question is admirably stated in a single sentence of Porphyry's *Isagoge*. It is perhaps cumbrous and involved, nor does it yield all the richness of its treasure at the bidding of a single cursory glance. But it had a really vital effect upon the course of history.

> Concerning *genera* or species, the question indeed whether they have substantial existence, or whether they consist in bare intellectual concepts only, or whether if they have a substantial existence they are corporeal or incorporeal, and whether they are separable from the sensible properties of the things (or particulars of sense) or are only in those properties and subsisting about them, I shall forbear to determine.[1]

This sentence does not look epoch-making; but it is. It is vital in history; and in philosophy it is a compressed statement of the terms of its greatest problem. It has even been said by one philosopher-theologian, Dean Rashdall, who was not given to facile enthusiasms, that outside the pages of the *Bible* there was no single sentence in all literature with more widespread and permanent effects on life and thought.

But to his statement of this unresolved problem, Porphyry adds a pendant. "A question of this kind," he says, "is a very deep one, and one that requires a long investigation." One is eager to regard that as a friendly hint, and to take it as such. For only those who have spent a lifetime in philosophic study can venture in safety on these deep and troubled waters. By those who can make no such claims, they are best left unfished.

[1] Tr. Hastings Rashdall, *Universities of Europe in the Middle Ages*, vol. i, p. 39. (Oxford University Press.)

For the twelfth-century dialecticians, however, these waters were the waters of life; and by their subtlety in ranging over them on the wings of argument their skill was judged. Let a master stumble over his interpretation of the nature of universals; let his pupils harry him by their eager questions into retracting his opinions, and at once his star had begun to wane. Unless he could recover his ground, and that swiftly, his star set to rise no more, but to bow to the star of his successful opponent.

V

Paris, when Abelard came through its gate in 1100, was a walled city. Like the London of the same period, it was at the beginning of the transitional date when stone took the place of timber for building purposes. Most of the houses were wooden erections of two or three stories, each jutting out above the other, and darkening the narrow cobbled pavement in the alley below. The streets were unlit and dirty. In hard winters marauding packs of wolves forced their way in; and, the gates being shut behind them, the people hunted them down, and used their skins "to wrap the baby bunting in."

The city was still without anything that could be called a university. But it was the Athens of twelfth-century Europe, for on the island of the Seine it possessed the episcopal cathedral school of Notre

Dame, the most famous school in Europe. It was a
magnet which lured half the ambitious scholars of
Europe from their homes. The streets were thronged
by young men, who had trudged there, many of them
begging their bread by the way. They came not only
from France, but also from Germany, England, and
far-distant Italy. Half the writers of the century are
full of stories of their poverty, their gay recklessness;
and the typical figure of twelfth-century literature is
the Paris student sitting in the tavern, dicing his
clothes away, and then satisfying a rapacious landlady
by singing scurrilous verses for pennies, or carrying
holy water to houses of sickness. They came to seek
learning and fortune—in that age nearly synonymous
—some to become great churchmen, others poets and
masters, and many to fall by the way. They were
drawn to Paris by the greatness of Notre Dame's
reputation, but also by the renown of its master,
William of Champeau, whose lectures on the Realism
of Plato, and whose denunciations of the nominalist
tendencies to heresy, had a far-flung fame.

The scanty buildings of the school adjoined the
cathedral; and the lecture rooms opened off a cloister
near the bishop's house. The lessons given there
consisted for the most part of lectures, followed by
discussion, which took the form of either the pro-
pounding of some metaphysical trap, or a commentary
upon some of the more obscure passages of Scripture,
or such of the works of Aristotle and Plato as were then
known. The scholars, clustered round the master's
chair, stood listening, the more quick-witted of them

eagerly waiting the chance to question some *dictum*
of the master. And among then stood Peter Abelard,
listening eagerly enough to this William of whom he
had heard so much, but destined to fight a long, bitter
·duel with him, and, in defeating him, to attract so
many scholars to Paris by the exhilaration of his
eloquence, that it became necessary to multiply masters,
to protect their privileges, to organise the scholars into
Nationes, and to evolve slowly (but not until after his
death) all the intricate mechanism of a university.

VI

William of Champeau was one of the most famous
men in Europe. He was the archdeacon of Paris. He
held one of the two most coveted of all educational
positions, the mastership of the school of Notre Dame.
He was one of the stalwarts of the unbendingly orthodox, and had served his cause well by making of scholasticism a captive maiden to the Israel of theology. To
this end he had evolved a new and a famous logical
formula upon which the Nominalists had shattered
their spears in vain. It was largely due to him, and his
undoubted dialectical brilliance, that the straiter sects
of the Realists were defeating their opponents on
their own ground; and his extreme rigidity in this
matter was counted to him for superabundance of
intelligence. His name it was which drew the scholars
to Paris, and by 1100 many of the first generations of

his pupils were occupying distinguished positions in various parts of Europe, and never tired of singing their master's praises.

There was another school in the city, on the hill of St Geneviève, just outside the wall, but in no sense could it be seriously considered as a rival to the cathedral school of Notre Dame. William, in fact, was as nearly without rivals as a man may be. Roscelin might perhaps have endangered his position, but he had been silenced, and his teaching discredited. That he had been allowed to creep back to France at all had been due to the grace and mercy of William's friends, and he was therefore certainly safe from any competition from Touraine. Moreover, the Church's ban on Roscelin had been pronounced mainly at the instigation of Anselm, the great abbot of Bec; and Anselm, once William's master, was now his most powerful patron and friend.

But a man without rivals is a man in a dangerous position. He can afford to ignore the enmity of such small spirits as are consumed by jealousy at the sight of talents they can never hope to possess. But the temptation of arrogance, never far from anyone, lies especially near to the famous and the powerful, and to this temptation William had fallen victim not once but many times. In the year 1100 no one stood near his chair, but many were smarting under the arrogance of his manner and the lash of his tongue, and awaited a chance of revenge. No doubt he was fully aware of his unpopularity with many of the more influential citizens of Paris. But did it greatly matter? There he sat, unchallenged, in his seat at the head of the greatest school in Europe, not even Chartres excepted; and there behind him loomed the portentous figure of Anselm, and the serried ranks of half the French bishops. These, together with his magnificent new formula, were surely sufficient guarantee against censure or intrigue. He was right. They could save him from censure and guard him from intrigue. But there were other ways of felling trees.

To William of Champeau and his school in the precincts of Notre Dame now resorted the most brilliant and perverse of all his pupils. Abelard quickly outstripped his fellow scholars. William was delighted. He commended the young man for his quickness of intellect and the capaciousness of his memory. By his fellows he was held remarkable for his depth of knowledge, and for his handsome and infectious gaiety. That his knowledge should be deeper than theirs was not remarkable. For he had had the advantage of being trained from the days of his infancy in letters by his admirable father, and of having studied under Roscelin himself.

But Abelard had reverence neither for age nor authority as such, and the day very soon came when he began to question whether William's fame as a dialectician was based upon a subtlety quite so deep as he had been led to suppose. It seemed that the very arguments he had learned from Roscelin could be used with surprising effect against William. It was true that he had decided that Nominalism, at any rate as it was expounded by Roscelin, was a broken reed, and if William could be made to stumble by the use of arguments which Abelard had himself rejected, it would seem that he must be a teacher living to a large extent upon his reputation. As such he was fair game. The pupil who had once been the pride of William's heart now became the bane of his life. He questioned him; he openly attacked him; he daily caused him to stumble, to retract his opinions; not even the magic formula was sacrosanct against the gay, the scarcely concealed mockery of this impudent young man. Such temerity was not unnaturally resented by the master, but Abelard was quickly involved in the scandalised indignation of his senior scholars, for the twelfth-century scholar was as hide-bound by the fetish of seniority and its automatic and exclusive privileges as are students of to-day. Abelard was braving unpopularity from two sides. He spoke later of this enmity as the first of his calamities, but it was of his own making. Nor was it without compensation. If William and his senior scholars were at one in their resentment of his impudence, there were many more who took his side in the duel, which quickly became known and was discussed beyond the cloisters of the school itself.

For while Abelard might with some justice be accused of an unbecoming aggression and conceit, the fact remained that his challenge was both public and successful. William had faltered in his exposition of the great problem; he had been forced to retract his opinions. There were many who rejoiced that a worthy rival had at last been found; and when that rival aspired to the mastership of a school of his own, they admitted that such an aspiration was indeed unheard-of presumption, but were therefore the more prepared to exert what influence they could to see that his desire was gratified. For in the presumption lay the piquancy of the situation, the cream of the jest. The arrogant archdeacon was palpably in danger of losing his reputation owing to a mere boy's cleverness. Nor, under the circumstances, could he call up his reserves, Anselm and the bishops. It was David and Goliath over again. So they watched, with amusement, as Abelard, "presuming," as he said himself, "upon my talents beyond the capacity of my years," looked around to see where his school might be established. It was 1102, just two years after he had come to Paris.

Paris itself was closed to him in the capacity of a master with a school of his own, so long as William held his position. But there were other places not too far away. There was Melun, a town of considerable importance, lying twenty miles away on the Seine. It was the seat of a royal palace. He decided to go there, and to leave William of Champeau.

But William was not so easily left. The departure of Abelard from Paris would certainly not be insupportable, but nothing would be gained if he did not go much farther away than Melun. In Paris he was certainly a nuisance, even a menace—but not a competitor. Established in Melun, a bare twenty miles away, he would be potentially a most dangerous competitor. It required no great perspicacity to see the danger. William, whose generosity was never prodigal, put forth all his efforts to prevent the establishment of this new school, or, at the least, if established it must be, to have it removed many miles farther from Paris than Melun. But the arts of intrigue and lobbying were employed in vain. He might bluster, or manœuvre secretly, or appeal to the unwritten laws of academic etiquette which surrounded even then the appointment of masters, but the ugly fact remained that his sins of arrogance were coming home to roost. Abelard was young, handsome, gay, and an undoubted genius. Though they saw clearly enough that this young Breton was himself no miracle of humility, those whose will turned the scale took a perverse pleasure in championing him.

Thus Abelard realised his ambition, and had his school. He flourished exceedingly. The first round of his twelve years' duel with William of Champeau had brought him notoriety, and students flocked to hear what he had to say. Drawn no doubt by this notoriety, they yet remained to be taught by him, when the attraction of a *cause célèbre* had faded to some degree. He was already known as a man extremely subtle, and difficult to answer in argument. But his own age knew him best as a teacher. Whatever one may think about the tragedy by which the world knows him, or to whatever conclusions one may come about the real depth and originality of his thought, one thing is certain, that he was one of the two or three greatest teachers—using the term in its restricted sense—that have ever lived. Now for the first time he could show his real quality. When he wrote: "And from this beginning of my school so much did my name in the art of dialectic begin to be magnified that not only the repute of my fellow scholars, but that of the master himself began to decline, and was gradually extinguished," he was not exaggerating, though to exaggerate both his misfortunes and his successes was normally his habit. It was no more than the truth.

Melun had been an experiment, and the accommodation of the school was not great. The number of scholars outgrew it within a year or two. "Hence it came about," he wrote, "that, presuming more largely upon myself, I made haste to transfer my school to the town of Corbeil, which is nearer to the city of Paris, so that there opportunity might furnish more frequent contests of disputation." In this sentence Abelard bares his real motive for moving his school. Corbeil, it is true, was a town on the royal demesne, and therefore desirable. But it was ten miles nearer Paris than Melun, and therefore doubly desirable. For Abelard was certainly viewing his career at this time in the light of a personal conflict with William of Champeau, and in his character there was so strong an element of sheer pugnacity that he required actually to be involved in a contest, or to see himself as so involved, before he exercised his talents to the full extent of their power. He had, and not unreasonably, a grudge against William, and that motive certainly weighed with him. But what weighed very much more was that he had a far higher

opinion of his own powers than of those of his old
master. He was not foolish enough to deny all merit
to William. He called him in the *Historia Calamitatum* "a man pre-eminent, rightly and by common
repute." Only, he knew that as compared with
himself William, famous as he was, was none the less
a mediocrity. And he naturally resented that mediocrity's power to keep him out of Paris, except in the
capacity of a student at his own school.

In the meantime he could thunder at him, and
thundering is more effective from a distance of ten
than twenty miles, even if it be purely academic. So
to Corbeil he went, and his scholars with him. From
that royal stronghold he cast forth torrents upon
torrents of words against the teaching of his adversary.
But then Nature asserted herself. He had been con-
sistently overworking for some years, and was stricken
by severe illness. He was obliged to shut his school
and leave Corbeil. He went back to his parents and
his home at Palais, gradually to recover his strength,
and to disappear from the scene for two or three
years.

VII

In the meantime William of Champeau was toying
with the idea of retiring. He was getting old. He
had failed to silence Abelard, and he imagined himself
spending the years that remained to him in the exhausting clamour of a perpetual warfare of words.
For it was certain that Abelard would not relent.

But it is always hard for those who have held great positions for many years to retire from them, and to hand them over to the care of some younger man. William, too, found it hard to summon sufficient resolution really to quit the school of Notre Dame, the scene of all his triumphs. For several years now the idea had lain fallow in his mind, but had not been put into action. In 1108, however, he finally nerved himself to it.

He decided to spend his remaining years in the practice of the life of solitude and contemplation, and to that end he established a small congregation of regular clergy near the Abbey of St Victor, outside the walls of Paris. The retirement was not unexpected, but his choice of the solitude of the religious life was, and a considerable sensation among the clergy resulted. The uncharitable said that he undertook solitude less because it was the thorny path of discipline and mortification than because a bishopric might well be lying at the path's end. Abelard shared this opinion. But there is no proof, nor even a real likelihood, that this conversion to the religious life was dictated by ambition.

There is, however, ample reason for supposing that he found the life of solitude more irksome than he had supposed. But he did not abandon it until he was commanded to do so. At first all went well. His clergy were few, but enthusiastic. They held his retirement from so distinguished a position in the world, and his embrace of religion, in high honour. They praised his devotion, and the sacrifice he had made for religion's sake. This sacrifice was the more complete and meritorious, they said, in that he had abandoned a career by no means at an end, and which might well have approximated in rank to the most exalted position in the secular service of the king.

Hildebert, now Bishop of Mans, soon to be Archbishop of Tours, a prelate with a weighty reputation for judgment and learning, was of the same mind as they. He wrote to William to commend him warmly for his action, which, he said, was the wise and natural thing for a philosopher above all men to do, for "solitude is in very truth philosophy in practice." The bishop also suggested with some persistence that he should not altogether cease from teaching. Was it quite impossible that the vocations for the lives of contemplation and instruction should be combined? Could not William combine them in his own person? He could, and thus advised, he did. He would combine the best of both worlds, monastic and secular, and that at the express desire of episcopal authority. He was a Religious, for he lived in a community and practised the Rule; but his practice of it and his community life no longer debarred scholars, nor indeed the general public, from resorting to his lectures. Abelard seemed to have vanished since his illness two years before; the priests among whom he lived were restfully respectful and admiring; his school was crowded; his piety revered. He began to dream once more of his old unchallenged supremacy in dialectics, and to think that, after all, it might yet return.

But trouble was again near to him. As he was

lecturing one day in the year 1111, he looked around his audience, and there, to his horror, he suddenly caught sight of the tall, slim figure of Abelard. He had recovered from his illness, and had since been travelling to complete the cure. Then, being completely restored to health, he hastened back to Paris to pick up the threads of his career. He declared himself that he came back to William in order to learn rhetoric; but he lost no time in seeking the opportunity to challenge the master once more.

> Then, I returning to him . . . contrived by the clearest chain of argument to make him alter, nay, to shatter his former opinion with regard to universals. For he had been of this opinion touching the community of universals, that he maintained a thing as a whole to be essentially the same in each of its individuals, among which, forsooth, there was no difference in essence but only variety in the multitude of their accidents. He now so corrected this opinion that thereafter he proclaimed the thing to be the same not essentially but indiscriminately. And inasmuch as this has always been the main question among dialecticians concerning universals . . . after he had corrected and then perforce abandoned his opinion, with such neglect did his instruction fall that he was scarcely admitted to be a teacher of dialectic at all.

That is a cumbrous, an inelegant passage from the *Historia Calamitatum*; but it is none the less a triumph song, and the scene to which it refers was dramatic, even though the stage was a lecture-room rather than a battlefield, and the weapons not swords but arguments and wits. For it was on that occasion that Abelard, renewing the duel in the restored fullness of his vigour, finally worsted his master.

The scene has been admirably described by Rémusat in his *Vie d'Abelard*. William, supposing Abelard was far away, was considerably disconcerted to see so suddenly his young rival in his audience. But he could hardly dismiss him, and he grimly set himself to continue his exposition of the principles of uncompromising Realism with as little visible chagrin as he could muster.

"Universals," he said, "are real essences and have positive reality. The Universal is one and the same: it resides in each creature, and forms a common foundation for them all. Thus, for instance, Humanity denotes the totality of human beings, but it is much more than a name given to all the individuals of the human race. It is a real essence, common to all, complete in each."

At this point, Abelard burst in, crying eagerly, "If Humanity is the basic essence of every man, then individuality itself is an Accident. Thus, when Plato is at Rome and Socrates at Athens, the aforesaid essence, Humanity, is embodied in its completeness in Plato in Rome and also in Socrates in Athens. So it seems that the Universal, Humanity, being the essence of the individual, is itself the individual, and it consequently carries the individual about with it wherever it goes. Thus, when Plato is in Rome, there too is Socrates, and when Socrates is in Athens, Plato is with him and in him." To this William could find no real answer. He took refuge in distinctions and qualifications, and, when again pressed, lapsed into stuttering unintelligibility.

In the margin of the copy of Rémusat's book in one of our great libraries, opposite the lines which describe Abelard's argument, some hasty, and perhaps weary student has pencilled the word TRIVIAL. To many it may seem so essentially academic as to deserve the epithet. But Rémusat has a surer eye. He says of it, *"C'était cette question fameuse et rédoutée qui avait perdu Roscelin."* And now William of Champeau had been added to its victims. He might still intrigue against Abelard, but—no one doubted it—he had met his final defeat. Now "he was scarcely admitted to be a teacher of dialectic at all," said Abelard, and justly.

It was the decisive engagement of the twelve years' war. But decisive engagements do not necessarily end wars immediately. Before peace can come the enemy must not only be vanquished, but must admit his defeat. So it was in this duel of intellects. William had in fact suffered defeat, but he was far from admitting it. He peered about for an opportunity of regaining yet once more his damaged prestige.

An opportunity for renewing the struggle quickly presented itself. William's successor in the school of Notre Dame resigned his position in Abelard's favour, for he found that as against the competition of the famous duel he could attract no pupils. He even enrolled himself among the scholars who resorted to Abelard immediately he began to lecture at Notre Dame. It was an open slight, and it was altogether too much for William's pride. In decency, he could hardly attack Abelard himself, but he could and did make the most outrageous accusations against the luckless master who had abdicated in his favour. He claimed, not without justice, that the hastiness and irregularity of the new appointment was sufficient to nullify it. He proceeded to lodge a formal complaint. Whether it was owing to the extreme vehemence with which William pressed his accusations, or to the skill he showed in harping upon the theme of the irregularities of the appointment, he won his case. The luckless befriender of Abelard was censured; Abelard was deposed; and his place William was allowed to fill by the nomination of some colourless friend of his own, whose name has not survived. He had apparently regained some of his old prestige for the moment, and Abelard had to return to Melun.

But this success was slight and momentary. Abelard had been forced to retire to Melun, but William had dealt a grievous blow to his reputation. That his tactics were inspired by jealousy and pride could hardly be doubted. The very vehemence with which they had been pursued proclaimed it. The disinterestedness of his monastic professions began to be openly doubted. Even his adherents at St Victor were murmuring. There was only one way by which the situation could yet be saved. In the profession of dialectics it was plain even to himself that he now had no future. He must leave Paris again, and take with him his devoted congregation of regular clergy, whilst their numbers were still undepleted. If such a retreat meant that he was opening the door to Abelard, well, it could not be helped. Thus William retired from the schools for the second time in 1112.

Abelard, who had kept himself well informed, immediately returned. William's nominee was still in possession of the School of Notre Dame, so Abelard set up his horn as master of the school on the hill of St Geneviève, outside the wall, and there, as was his invariable experience, he attracted vast crowds of scholars. He was in fact, if not in theory, the supreme teacher in Paris, for such was his success that the unlucky master at Notre Dame was forced to demonstrate the futility of his patron by talking learnedly in an empty room.

This news was carried to William, who, roused yet again to fury by his pupil's success, once more changed his mind, gathered his disciples round him, and advanced on Paris for battle. The stage was set for a great occasion, a resounding final fight.

It is with a certain sadness that one watches these preparations for a struggle which must inevitably end in the defeat, and, because it was wantonly provoked, in the dishonour of an old and once great man. The truth is that William was temperamentally incapable of understanding that a young man, one of his own pupils, might be his intellectual superior. A long experience of uncontested authority, of eager adulation, had blinded him. Abelard saw only the infuriating figure of an elderly and jealous man, living on his reputation, and embodying all that youth finds irritating in age. There was pity in the spectacle, but he missed it; and in remembering only the desperate and hardly honourable efforts made against himself, he saw in William only a very proper target for his shafts of wit, and his accusations of unrelieved malignity.

The last engagement between the pair now began. Abelard thundered from St Geneviève, and William from St Victor. Challenges flew backwards and forwards between the rival schools. But the end was already decided, and events moved towards it inexorably, for daily Abelard gained the pupils whom William lost. But the climax was to be less spectacular than the setting of the stage had suggested. For just when events were pointing to the staging of one final mighty scene of conflict for the edification of Paris, Abelard received news which made him leave Paris forthwith.

VIII

The news was a message from his mother in Palais. Whilst her son had been immersed in his controversies, she and her husband, Berenger, having finished what they considered was their work in the world, the upbringing and education of their children, had decided that they would spend the evening of their days in withdrawal from the world. They would become professed, and would enter houses of religion. In the Middle Ages such a course was perfectly usual among deeply religious people, for monasticism was in the air they breathed. Nobody saw any reason for surprise, nor were attempts made to dissuade them.

Berenger had already departed to a monastery; but Lucy, his wife, lingered in her home until her eldest son could come to her, and she could take her leave of him. She sent for him; and he, immersed in the conflict as he then was, immediately and without hesitation departed from Paris and hastened to Palais. It was a simple, ordinary leave-taking to which he had been summoned; and yet it had the greatest import-ance. For it was a turning-point in his life, than which few were to be more important.

Lucy's delay to follow her husband until she had seen her son was possibly due to hidden and deliberate motives. Berenger had carefully nourished in him the signs of an aptitude for letters. That had been his gift: now Lucy was to bestow hers. And her gift was—religion. What happened during the few days Abelard spent with his mother before she finally retired to her convent is naturally unknown in any detail. But when he left her he was different. The religious motif had now entered his life and become a part of it. For many years it was not to exercise any very noticeable influence upon his character; but though he seemed to be the same pugnacious young genius he had been before, there was none the less a subtle difference. His nature had gained a poise, a sense of proportion, which, operating slowly and fitfully at first, yet became increasingly influential upon his actions and thought as the years rolled away. Nor was there as yet any immediate and marked sign of the consciousness of dedication, but that too was to come, and to strengthen him by enabling him to

regard his conflict with St Bernard and his friends as a
Holy War.

Lucy had planted the seed, and wisely left it to grow
of itself. But she had exacted one promise, that he
would go at once to the great school at Laon and there
study theology under Anselm. If she had been thinking only of the greatness of his career she could have
compelled him to no course more likely to contribute
to it. A knowledge of theology and theological
method was the only serious gap in his equipment;
and in an age when the only field open to all ambitious
young men was the service of the Church, ignorance
of the science of sciences was a crippling limitation.
Perhaps Abelard himself felt this.

As soon as he had bade his mother farewell and had
seen her professed, as she desired, he hastened again
to Paris. There he found already in being the very
situation for which he had been fighting for twelve
years. William had quitted the scene—this time
irrevocably, for he had at least been given the honour
that was his due. He had been made Bishop of
Chalons, and, happy at last to find an external release
from the exhausting brawling towards which his
pride had compelled him, had departed to his diocese
in Marne, whilst Abelard was still in Brittany. There
he found the love once more he had so sadly
missed; and when he died, seven years later, he was
mourned by all his clergy, who had revered him for
his piety, and loved him for his unfailing readiness to
help them in their troubles and difficulties. He became,
too, an intimate friend to Bernard of Clairvaux, then

a young abbot; and he was the first, no doubt, to make known to that redoubtable saint the activities of his young adversary.

At last the field was clear for Abelard, and he had achieved his ambitions. Paris was an adoring city, only waiting for him to enter and take triumphant possession. He did enter, but he did not stay. He passed straight through the city and resolutely made his way to Laon, twenty miles or more to the east.

Anselm's school at Laon, where he now sought admission, was the most famous academy of its kind in Europe. Its fame, however, was due to the remarkable man who was at its head. Anselm's reputation was continental. For many years now he had been teaching theology, and the bishops and priests who had been his pupils were widely scattered over Europe. His learning was vast; but his temperament was intensely conservative. No one was more deeply familiar with every word the Fathers had written, and he knew the whole Bible almost by heart. But his mind moved within these vast but none the less circumscribed limits. These, to him, were theology's formularies. They were there—given, and no additions could be made. Commentary was praiseworthy, but criticism impious. They enjoyed plenary inspiration, and, by their nature it did not fall within the competence of human reason to add to, or even, in certain circumstances, to explain the Faith once for all delivered. His method of instruction was to take some book of the Bible, and to comment exhaustively on its every word. It may sound far from exhilarating, but, by common consent, all who heard him were entranced both by what he said and by his manner of saying it. He was a superb orator. His eloquence was indeed so persuasive that its very charm made Abelard suspect that his golden periods hid a serious confusion of meaning. He steeled himself against succumbing to the honeyed words; and he began ruthlessly to analyse them. The result was that once more he uncovered a false reputation, and wrote, "He was admirable in the eyes of his hearers, but of no account in the sight of questioners. His fluency of words was admirable, but in a sense they were contemptible and devoid of reason."

Abelard, strong in the compulsion of his new-born religious impulse, had deliberately abjured the Paris triumph which was prepared for him, and had put himself to school again. He might well find boys at Laon whom he had himself taught in Paris only a few months before. Now, by his own act, at the age of thirty-four, he had put himself on a level with them.

But, in practice, he could not undo the past; nor could he for very long remain contentedly a young student once more. His age and his experience both forbade it. He was not then, or at any time, at all susceptible to the atmosphere of prestige which surrounds fame or old age. When he found that Anselm either stumbled over his questions or angrily refused to answer on the ground that only impiety could put such questions, he mentally dismissed him as being no more than an eloquent exponent of ortho-dox, but hopelessly unimaginative theology. He was

disappointed and disillusioned, and, perversely, he
fanned this state of mind into a strange temper. His
remarks about Anselm were indecently discourteous,
and in later years he was content to set down on paper
this patently incomplete judgment.

> When he kindled a fire he filled his house with smoke,
> rather than lighted it with the blaze. His tree, in full
> life, was conspicuous from afar to all beholders, but by
> those who stood near and diligently examined the same
> it was found to be barren. To this tree therefore, when
> I had come that I might gather fruit from it, I understood
> that it was the fig-tree which the Lord cursed, or that old
> oak to which Lucan compares Pompey, saying—
>
> > There stands the shadow of a mighty name,
> > Like to a tall oak in a fruitful field.

But such charlatans as fit this condemnation are
hardly held in honour by their old pupils in every part
of Europe. It is plainly so much less than the truth that
one is driven to wonder why Abelard felt so bitterly
against Anselm. But the implied question cannot be
satisfactorily answered. Abelard's motives are difficult
enough to discover when we have good and full
evidence to guide us. But here we have only what
he tells us.

His anger swiftly became contempt, and his contempt was reflected in his conduct. He began to
attend his lectures less and less regularly. This
method of protest is not unknown in a modern
university; but whereas nowadays one's tutor becomes
the avenging Nemesis, then other scholars, themselves
in statu pupillari, dealt with the situation. For frequent
absence from the lectures was considered to be more

an insult to the lecturer than a breach of discipline.
The other scholars, imagining that Anselm's honour
lay in their hands, took him to task. They were led
by two friends, who were to become bitter and lifelong
enemies of Abelard's, Alberic of Rheims and Lotulph
of Novara. Alberic's expostulations naturally had no
effect upon Abelard. He remained impenitent.

Then, one day, the conversation in the school
turned upon a topic which is perennial in all theological colleges, the relationship between "secular"
and "sacred" learning. There were those who held
that the man of God should regard the knowledge of
the secular arts and sciences as forbidden to him.
Others held that literature should be allowed to be
studied, but, of course, in strict moderation. The
straiter spirits bridled a little: how, for instance, could
their laxer brethren affirm that a knowledge of literature was of any advantage to their true business of
interpreting the Scriptures?

Abelard was standing by, and this remark annoyed
him. He promptly pointed out that he had already
considerable knowledge of secular learning, and that
he had found it of the utmost value in reading the
Scriptures. Nay, more, the Scriptures could not be
understood at all without a preliminary knowledge of
literature. He spoke oracularly: and his words were
promptly interpreted as a challenge. The conserva-
tives were swift to take it up. They bade him prove
his words. Now Abelard was never the man to refuse
a challenge, though he had not meant to be so understood. He told them to test him as they would;

he would show them he was right. They conferred for a moment; and then told him that he must convince them of the truth of his statements by lecturing on no less a master of obscurity than the prophet Ezekiel. His only reply was to bid them all attend his lecture the very next day. His promptitude staggered them. They said "that in so weighty a matter there was nothing to be gained by haste, but that seeing my inexperience I must give longer thought to the strengthening of my exposition. But I indignantly replied that it was not my custom to advance by practice but rather by intelligence; and added that either I abandoned the contest altogether, or they must come to my lecture without delay."

In all his life Abelard accomplished few feats of greater brilliance. The morrow dawned, and he repaired to the chosen place, to find a mere handful there to hear him. It was natural, for it seemed quite ridiculous that he could lecture on an unfamiliar subject at such short notice. The few who had come were there to laugh. No atmosphere could be more wholly unsympathetic. But he began, and soon the tittering ceased. Before the end those who had come to laugh listened spellbound; and when it was over they begged him to continue in earnest what had been started in a fit of bravado. He lectured again and yet again to an ever-increasing audience; but before he could finish the course he had planned he was suddenly forbidden to continue.

The sheer brilliance of this feat was hardly likely to appease Alberic and those of his party among the

Laon scholars. They had thought to make him look ridiculous; and they were now seething with fury at his gay and successful impertinence. Angrily they went to Anselm, and obtained from him an order that this usurping of his position must cease at once. According to the unwritten rules of etiquette he should never have placed himself in such a position, for there was a binding rule that before a student could begin to teach, his master's sanction had to be obtained. Abelard's breach of this rule may seem purely technical, but Alberic and his friends remembered it, and, years afterwards, introduced it into the indictment drawn against him at the Council of Soissons.

This storm of trivialities decided him. He was wasting his time at Laon. Anselm seemed to have nothing to teach him; and would now make his life impossible in his school. Suddenly he departed from Laon, and returned to Paris. There he had not been forgotten. The mastership of the school of Notre Dame was vacant: he was immediately appointed, and, in addition, on his taking minor orders, a canonry of the cathedral was bestowed on him. His hour of triumph had come. Characteristically, he inaugurated his régime by finishing his interrupted course of lectures on *Ezekiel*.

IX

He had done well to postpone his triumph by serving his term at Laon. For when he returned to Paris he found that his already tremendous reputation as a dialectician was reinforced by rumours of his equal proficiency in theology. Such knowledge of theology as he possessed had not, however, been gained from Anselm. So much he himself admitted. But though his stay at Laon had been short it had not been barren. He had at least added to his equipment a knowledge of the method of theological study, and he was both learned and brilliant enough to teach himself when the method of study had once been mastered. Moreover, he had no sooner been faced by the new method —for it was new to him—than he had at once suggested radical improvements in it, and had immediately proceeded to put his improvements into practice, adding thereby to his reputation as *Malleus Monachorum*.

By now he was accustomed to success; but the success which greeted his return to Notre Dame far surpassed anything which even he had previously known. It was quite phenomenal. He was the sensation of his time. Every contemporary authority, whether friend or foe, tells the same tale. If we look in St Bernard's letters, or in the Chronicle of Bishop Otto of Friesingen, or the *Metalogicus* of the cool-headed John of Salisbury, or in the records of the convent of Morigny, or in the biographies of those who were to be his enemies; or if we piece together the chance and scattered remarks to be found in the lesser works of the century, the tale is always the same. In Paris there was reigning a master supremely great, who exercised a fascination quite unprecedented over the minds and hearts of his pupils. He drew them

young and old, clerks and laymen from all parts of
Europe. Very soon he had a following of five
thousand scholars, a tremendous number for that time.
They burst the cramped limits of Notre Dame, and by
their wildness they created many scenes of chaos in the
Paris streets. Every account of them tells of their
abject poverty; but they managed to beg, borrow,
steal, or gamble the money for their schools' fees.
Abelard quickly became as wealthy as he was famous.

The secret of his success lay not in the depth of his
learning, which has been authoritatively questioned,
but in the manner of his teaching. He was what is
called a "born teacher"; and born teachers are often
less erudite than Regius Professors. But in spite of
the sensation it caused, we have little direct knowledge
of this method. From Abelard himself we have none,
for he always laboured under the delusion that his
prodigious learning and subtlety alone accounted for
his popularity. There are, however, stray stories,
and nicknames, which have come drifting down the
centuries, and indicate fairly clearly the excitement
which was always present in the room when he was
lecturing. He was called by one writer Goliath; and
again in another context, Proteus, "flashing from
philosophy to poetry, from poetry to wild jesting:
a scholar with the wit of a jongleur, and the graces of
a *grand seigneur*." [1] He would begin a lecture by
expounding the contradictory fallacies of Nominalism
and Realism; then break off with some sarcastic
ribaldry about the intelligence, so-called, of a Roscelin,

[1] Helen Waddell, *The Wandering Scholars*, p. 108.

a William of Champeau, or a Jocelyn of Douai who
continued to hold opinions which he had clearly
demonstrated to be ridiculous, whereat the room
would ring with spontaneous laughter; and then,
easily checking it, he would plunge into the subtleties
of his own *via media*, Conceptualism. He would
vary the aridity of his philosophical and theological
disquisitions by employing daring and vivid metaphors
drawn from the classical poets, Virgil or Ovid, or
from the ballads of the Troubadours which he had
learned during his wanderings, leaving the scholars
radiant with an awful delight at the idea of a Trouba-
dour's ballad being used to illustrate a nice point of
theology. The scholar who went to him for instruction was certain that he would be led into very deep
waters, but that the leading would be gaily performed,
and with constant exhilaration.

But it is in the nickname *Rhinoceros Indomitus* that
there lies the most fertile hint of the secret of his
success. His room was not only one in which
laughter and hard thinking and the beauty of great
oratory perpetually followed each other. It was also
in some sort a battlefield. People came to challenge
his arguments, or he issued resounding challenges to
masters in other schools to open debate. There was
always the sense of conflict in the air; and though the
excitement of a conflict is hardly calculated to further
the cool dispassionateness necessary to exact scholarship, there is no doubt that it banishes boredom. To
gain an audience in such means may not be morally
commendable, but there is no doubt that the means

are effective. While it would hardly be an exact and comprehensive statement of fact to say that Abelard deliberately resorted to pugnacity as a means of increasing the number of his scholars, there is no doubt that the pugnacity which was so strong an element in his teaching had precisely that effect.

As the term *Rhinoceros Indomitus* implies, the glamour of conflict was in his blood. Possibly it was hereditary, for his family came from that rank of society to whom fighting was as their daily bread. But whether hereditary or not, it was certainly there; and without it he would have been only half as effective. His was one of those natures which need the salt of conflict to urge them to their greatest efforts. But the element of pugnacity presupposes another quality— self-reliance; and his self-reliance, which is stamped all over such a nickname as *Rhinoceros Indomitus*, was robust enough to win him fame such as few men have enjoyed, but in the end it brought him to ruin.

To his natural gift for teaching he added a very considerable equipment of knowledge. Of the arts of dialectic and metaphysics he was a master. He lived in an age when it was possible for one mind to master all the philosophic *data* that was available, and he had mastered it. He was extremely well read, as his fluency of quotation shows. He could, with equal readiness, turn to the translations of Aristotle and Plato, the writings of Boethius, Porphyry, Macrobius, the Early Fathers, and the classical authors, Ovid, Virgil, Priscian, and Cicero. From this comprehensive school he had learned not only philosophical method, but he had also won a great proficiency in the art of self-expression by word and pen. He was a stylist. None knew better than he how to effect a synthesis of the gleanings of these varied fields and how to weave the one study into the other, to make poetry illustrate theology.

But he had definite limitations. Mathematics was a closed book. Beyond the common philosophic terms he knew little Greek, and no Hebrew. His training in theology under Anselm had been decidedly sketchy. But a limitation far more serious than any mere gaps in his knowledge was his headstrong temperament, and his constant inability to do anything with opposition except to charge at it blindly and recklessly. The word conciliation was unknown in his vocabulary, so that every encounter only raised a fresh set of implacable enemies, whose defeat did not help them to forget the rough handling they had received. Every day he added fresh drops to the vials of wrath stored up against him, and the day was to come when they were all emptied upon his head.

This fatal inability was particularly clearly shown in the story of young Gosvin of Douai, who, greatly daring, aspired to play the David to his Goliath, and who came to Paris when Abelard was at the height of his power to challenge him in debate. The story has importance not only because Gosvin was destined to intervene again in that stormy life, but also because it gives us a first-hand glimpse of Abelard among his adoring pupils.

Gosvin was a scholar at Jocelyn's school at Douai.

Jocelyn had for some time been bearing the brunt of
Abelard's sarcasm on account of the watered variety
of nominalism which he held. Gosvin was the best
of his scholars, and when they decided that for the
honour of the school and its master *Rhinoceros Indomitus* must be bearded in his den, it was he who was
chosen to sustain the encounter. His master tried
to dissuade him. He told him that Abelard "cavils
rather than disputes; is more of a jester than a doctor.
He is pertinacious in his errors; and if the truth does
not lie on his side of the argument he will never
acknowledge it." But such persuasions were urged
in vain. Gosvin took several of his friends, and
departed to Paris, supported by the hopes and the
prayers of his school. He was a young champion,
more than seven years younger than Abelard.

He came at length to the room in which the famous
master was lecturing, a small, slight, shabbily dressed,
but pleasing figure, and was allowed to sit down with
his friends. He was not long silent. Abelard got
thoroughly into his stride, when suddenly Gosvin
interrupted to ask a question. Abelard, checked in
full gait, was not pleased. He glared at Gosvin,
"disdainfully and menacingly," and roughly bade him,
"hold your tongue and don't interrupt my lecture."
But Gosvin had not come all the way to Paris to hold
his tongue. He protested, and was backed in his
protests by his friends. For some time they could
get no reply. But at last Abelard shrugged his
shoulders, and said, "Well, speak then, if you have
anything to say." The question (what question we do

not know) was put, and the argument began. Gosvin pressed his adversary to such good purpose that eventually he involved him in an absurdity. Abelard was left shaking with impotent wrath, while Gosvin, having triumphantly achieved his temerarious purpose, went on his way rejoicing.

So, at least, the story goes. But it is told by a monk of the monastery over which Gosvin was one day to rule as abbot. It is thus partisan, and there is no supporting evidence of its truth or its freedom from exaggeration. Whether true, or half true, the alleged defeat made little difference to Abelard. Gosvin had done well, and had made a name for himself. He was one day to found a famous school of his own in his native Douai, and eventually he was to be canonised. But he had not conquered Abelard. Abelard was not invulnerable, but someone stronger than Gosvin was needed to find his Achilles' heel.

For neither Abelard's fame nor his popularity was in the least abated. Whatever the exact truth of this episode may be, it is certain that it was no more than an episode, and that it had no lasting significance. Abelard continued in his fame and in the number of his pupils. With his name one could conjure inside and outside his school. For when he was born, the good fairies had clouded the sky and jostled each other in their eagerness to present him with their impalpable gifts. He was physically beautiful. He was naturally energetic—though his energy was lightened and made socially tolerable by timely affectations of lassitude, for it suited him well to be deemed able to scale all

heights without apparent effort. He was gay and
pleasant in manner, in spite of his enemies' charges to
the contrary, and his gaiety and charm were only made
the more apparent by the gravity and harshness which
sometimes obscured them. To be in his company was
felt to be an honour; to revel in the intoxication of
his eloquence was to be envied, for, as an enemy wrote,
"He is sublime in eloquence." His renown in Paris
was such that the women, leaving their tasks when he
passed by, crowded to the doors of their houses, and
the children pressed their noses to the windows of the
upper rooms to see the man whose exploits were the
table talk of their elders. Many years later Heloise
wrote to him:

> For who among kings or philosophers could equal
> thee in fame? What kingdom or city or village did not
> burn to see thee? Who, I ask, did not hasten to gaze
> upon thee when thou appearedst in public, nor on thy
> departure with straining neck and fixed eye follow thee?
> What wife, what maiden did not yearn for thee in thine
> absence nor burn in thy presence? What queen or
> powerful lady did not envy me my joys?

It was no more than the sober truth. And if by the
ecclesiastical and secular society of Paris he was
admired, and his presence coveted, by his pupils he
was loved, and that love he never lost. Life was to
lead him into disgrace and utter misfortune, but he
never lost his hold upon the imagination of youth,
nor upon the devotion of those he had once taught.
Scholars would come to him as readily in a lonely
mountain cave as they did in Paris, and wherever
Abelard was there was his school.

At last, then, he was triumphant, the unquestioned monarch of his own world. He owed his position to no one but himself, and he had attained it early in life. For the next three or four years his life lay in Paris among his scholars. Should he tire of the school, there seemed no ambition too wild or chimerical to be entertained. In the Church's service was real equality of opportunity. There was only one thing needful—ordination to the priesthood, for, though a canon, he was only in minor orders—and then there was no end to the great posts to which he could legitimately aspire, nor to the dreams, never far from his heart, of being a pioneer in the work of bringing reason to the service of religion. But for all that there was time and to spare. He was calm and happy. He knew that permanent quiescence in however exalted a position was alien to his nature. But for the present all was peace, and he could contentedly eat the lotus flower of fame and popularity.

But he had failed to take one factor into his calculations—the niece of one of his fellow canons of Notre Dame. As it all turned out, these years were his heyday, his only experience of peace and calm. Soon their peace was shattered by the disturbing presence of Heloise, who brought with her the gifts of immortality, irretrievable disaster, and ruin.

X

Heloise was a girl of eighteen, living alone with her uncle, Canon Fulbert of Notre Dame, in a house in the

Rue des Chantres, near the cathedral. Her parents had died when she was but a child, and they had left her penniless. It is said that they had both belonged to ancient and noble families; and some writers have tried to trace her lineage, though they have had little success. Her uncle had taken her in, and to him she owed her upbringing and education. He had sent her to the Benedictine convent at Argenteuil, where the nuns had taught her. When she returned to Paris, Fulbert, who lived in an atmosphere of scholarship, and was himself a fine classicist, had taught her, and had delighted in so doing, for she was such a pupil as all teachers dream of.

The Argenteuil nuns and Fulbert had between them worked wonders, for there was no girl or woman in Paris, and probably none in all Europe, who could approach the knowledge of Heloise. At the early age of eighteen it had already brought her fame. She habitually spoke and wrote in Latin; and in addition she could read in both Greek and Hebrew. In her letters she quoted with equal readiness and facility from the great classical writers and from the Church Fathers. In so doing she was not parading her erudition. She was writing to Abelard; and he knew it well enough already. Nor, in her three great letters, had she the heart to think of anyone or anything other than the tangled fortunes of herself and the man to whom she was writing. She was, in fact, the apotheosis of the well-read person, in that she could find in her reading an apt reflection of her every mood, and that without consciously searching for it. Whether she was speaking to Abelard and trying to dissuade him from marriage, or whether she wrote to reproach him for forgetting or neglecting to write to her, always the apt illustration from Seneca or Jerome, or some other, lay ready to her hand. It is not surprising that she enjoyed great fame in Paris whilst still a young girl, and that people referred to her as *La Très Sage Héloïse*.

In the eyes of her own contemporaries her chief distinction thus lay in the depth of her learning, and the vivacity with which she wore it. Physically, she was tall and fair. Her presence was striking, but her features, in spite of the assertions of the tradition, were not beautiful beyond the ordinary. Abelard himself most aptly stated the measure and cause of her reputation: "While in face she was not inferior to other women, in the abundance of her learning she was supreme. For inasmuch as this advantage, namely literary knowledge, is rare in women, so much the more did it commend the girl, and had won her the greatest renown throughout the realm."

In these days of the higher education of women the knowledge of Heloise would perhaps still be exceptional, but not sufficiently so to be generally remarked. But the intricate texture and the shining integrity of her mind would be highly remarkable in this or in any age.

The pattern of her mind is mirrored with an almost disconcerting frankness in her letters to Abelard, written in desperate and tragic circumstances, many years after they had parted. Her knowledge of herself was complete and exhaustive, but the introspection that knowledge involved was luminously free from any taint of morbidness. She did not fret or chatter about the necessity of finding and expressing her personality, but she had the old Greek facility for facing reality undismayed. When she wrote the letters which have come down to us she had every excuse for running away from the facts of her own character and circumstances. She was a nun—and she had no shadow of a nun's vocation. She was an abbess, finally professed and irretrievably committed. She had sole charge of the nuns in the Abbey of the Paraclete, a burden laid on her by both her husband and her bishop. She could not conceivably escape her vows of celibacy and seclusion. On that bed she had long lain, and there she must lie for all the years ahead. Who, similarly situated, would not pretend to a vocation? It was, one would think, the only way to make life tolerable. Abelard had taken precisely that refuge. Who, lacking a vocation, would not stoutly declare it was present, and come at last to believe in it by the ordinary processes of suggestion? Her passions had been tempestuous—they still were. Would she not be tempted, seeing that they could not be gratified, to exorcise them by declaring to others and seeking to persuade herself that these flames had become ashes—the ashes of regret? It was the rational way of escape. But for her it was treason against the shining candour of her mind, and she wrote:

In me these goads of the flesh, these incentives of lust (memories) the very fervour of my youth and my experience of the sweetest pleasures greatly stimulate, and all the more oppress me with their assaults the weaker the nature is that they are assaulting. They preach that I am chaste who have not discovered the hypocrite in me. They make the purity of the flesh into a virtue, when it is a virtue not of the body but of the mind. Having some praise among men, I deserve none before God. . . . I am judged religious at this time, in which but a little part of religion is not hypocrisy, when he is extolled with the highest praise who does not offend the judgment of men. . . .

But in the whole period of my life (God wot) I have ever feared to offend thee rather than God, I seek to please thee more than Him. Thy command brought me, not the love of God, to the habit of religion. See how unhappy a life I must lead, more wretched than all others, if I endure all these things here in vain having no hope of reward in the future. For a long time thou, like many others, hast been deceived by my simulation, so as to mistake hypocrisy for religion; and thus, strongly commending thyself to our prayers, what I expect of thee, thou demandest of me.

The letter from which this passage is taken is one of the most matchless and pathetic letters in the world. But whoever reads it for the first time will find that his dominant emotion is not pity, but sheer admiration for the courageous mind that would never hide the facts or seek to escape their starkness behind a sea of excuses. Even her lamentations are on Abelard's behalf. Her own plight was indeed wretched, but for her its wretchedness consisted chiefly in the knowledge of the disaster their love had brought upon Abelard.

This courage, capacity for sacrifice, and self-knowledge marked her out whilst she was still living with her uncle the quiet scholar's life into which the emotional chaos of passion never entered, and where the note was always the cool lucidity of the ordered life. The strange and tragic experience which awaited her did but accentuate qualities already present. They were qualities which made for clarity of purpose as of mind, and thus her motives are always clearly discernible, whereas Abelard's need a vast amount of disentanglement. Abelard and she differed most in that she was always luminously free from any trace of affectation or posing, whereas, until the last months of his life, he never ceased to erect and display phantasies of himself.

The story of their love has been lately told in a prose romance of unforgettable beauty by Mr George Moore, who makes of it what is undoubtedly one of the finest novels of our time. He takes, as of course he is perfectly justified in doing, the novelist's licence in regard to such matters as dates and motives; and where the facts are not clearly established, he naturally chooses whatever theory will best fit his pattern, and treats it as fact. Such a method is justified by its results, and a clearer picture emerges from it than from the historian's qualifications.

Abelard and Heloise were the two most celebrated personalities in Paris. How did they first meet? According to Mr Moore, Heloise was possessed by a deep desire to hear his famous lectures, and, with characteristic directness, she paid clandestine visits to his lecture room at Notre Dame. Soon she found that her heart as well as her brain was centred in him, and, after some hesitation, contrived to put herself in his path as he passed through the cathedral. It may be so, but it is surmise, and there are plainly difficulties about it.

But it is less improbable than Abelard's own account of it. For he, eager as always to convince himself and others that all his actions proceeded from a deliberate chain of reasoning and never from impulse—he, who was always the slave of impulse—wrote in the *Historia Calamitatum* as though he loved Heloise because he deliberately chose to do so. "Seeing in her, therefore, all those things which are wont to attract lovers, I thought it suitable to join her with myself in love."

He continues:

> So, being wholly inflamed with love for this girl, I sought an opportunity whereby I might make her familiar with me in daily and intimate conversation, and so the more easily lead her to consent. With which object in view, I came to terms with the aforesaid uncle of the girl, certain of his friends intervening, that he should take me into his house, which was hard by our school, at whatever price he might ask.

It is an excellent illustration of the harm that Abelard did himself when he wrote that unfortunate document. He wrote of Heloise as though he deliberately proposed, and treacherously contrived her ruin. Whatever the truth may be, it is not that. He was in a state of psychological abnormality when *Historia Calamitatum* was written. The memory of his love was one to which he showed no mercy, perhaps because he dared not, and he deceived himself.

Rémusat is wiser, who sums it up, "A noble and secret instinct bade him love her who had no equal."

Fulbert was tremendously ambitious for his niece's reputation as a scholar, and what better tuition could she have than that which Abelard would be likely to give? And, for so true a lover of learning as Fulbert, how delightful was the prospect of long uninterrupted talks with the most famous and stimulating scholar of his day! If he had any misgivings on the score of Abelard's spending several hours each day alone with Heloise, he was reassured by his reputation for strict chastity, though whether that was deserved is a debated point.

So whatever the truth may be about the approaches to the bargain, once it was broached it was quickly struck, and Abelard came to live in the house in the RUE DES CHANTRES, over the door of which was one day to be painted this sign:

HÉLOISE ABELARD HABITÈRENT CES LIEUX
DES SINCÈRES AMANS MODELES PRÉCIEUX.

His duties were to give Heloise several hours' instruction each day in philosophy and the Latin classics. Fulbert bade him that should she prove lazy or intractable he must at once beat her soundly—an eloquent comment on the scholastic methods of the age.

"What more need I say?" asked Abelard. "First in one house we are united, then in one mind." Their textbook was not *The Consolation of Philosophy* but *The Art of Love*; and, the opportunities being virtually unlimited, they loved in deed as in word. "No stage of love was omitted by us in our cupidity, and, if love could elaborate anything new, that we took in addition. The less experienced we were in these joys, the more ardently we persisted in them, and the less satiety did they bring us." The words are Abelard's, and they are an ample confession. The months went by; Fulbert seemed to be unsuspicious; and the lovers tarried in an ecstasy of abandon.

Yet neither was wholly actuated by lust. They were possessed by a love which demanded homage from their minds as from their bodies. Abelard's whole being was turned upon and centred in Heloise. The urgency of his creative necessity found its outlet in the composition of a stream of lyrics and ballads. But he had no energy left for his school. To lecture there became a weariness to his spirit, and he regarded his pupils jealously for their claims upon his time. Naturally his lectures quickly became dull and insipid. Relying on his facility of language, he did not prepare them, but was content to trust in the inspiration of the moment, and to dress in new words and phrases the matter of his old lectures and arguments, which he knew by heart. His scholars were puzzled and disappointed, until, at last, they discovered the reason. Then the secrecy of the intrigue was shattered. Scandal whispered swiftly in the streets, and the story, together with a host of exaggerations, became generally known. Abelard's ballads were sung in the Paris streets.

Fulbert had of course heard the rumour. People had been careful to let him know—they would be. At first he refused to believe, and kept his knowledge of the rumours to himself. After all, the situation was in any case one calculated to set scandalous tongues gossiping. But whereas unfounded scandal quickly dies away, this did not die. It increased in both volume and intensity, until Fulbert could no longer pretend ignorance, and he separated Abelard from his niece.

At this point Mr George Moore invents a conversation between Fulbert and Abelard, wherein Fulbert taxes him with the rumours, says that he does not himself believe that they are true, and asks him to deny them. Abelard does deny them; and Heloise, chancing to enter the room, substantiates his denial. For this story there is no evidence either in Abelard's own account of the matter—and he was in no mood to spare himself when he wrote—nor in Rémusat's *Life*. But lack of evidence does not prove its falsity. It seems incredible that Fulbert should have turned Abelard out of his house without giving any explanation or asking any questions. Whether Mr Moore is correct in his surmise cannot now be ascertained. One would certainly prefer to think his implied accusation false. But, supposing it to be true, it does supply a motive, inadequate, of course, as any motive must be, for the warped mind which led him into the wreaking of his hideous and insensate vengeance.

A more bitter trial than separation now approached, one which certified Fulbert in his suspicions. Heloise was with child. Faced with certain discovery, she characteristically refrained from bewailing her lot, but rather rejoiced. "With the greatest exultation," she at once wrote to Abelard, asking what he would have her do. He acted swiftly. He chose a night when her uncle was away from home, then came for her, and took her away with him to the refuge of his sister's home, near the castle of Clisson, in Brittany. There they stayed until Heloise gave birth to her child. It was a boy, and they gave him the curious name Astrolabe. For several weeks after the birth they stayed at Clisson, and found them all too short amid the peaceful loveliness of the countryside in that district.

But their flight had settled nothing. It had only raised fresh problems to add to the old, which, sooner or later, had to be faced by them both.

Fulbert, not unnaturally, was a stricken man. His sorrow was intense, but it was not unalloyed. There was in it the fury of an outraged pride as well as the sadness of a betrayed trust. Gradually the element in his emotion which was pride outweighed and displaced the sadness; and it was noticed that having at first been stricken with sorrow, he now became nearly demented by the violence of his rage. He began to turn over schemes in his mind whereby he might be revenged. He knew Abelard and he knew Heloise. The secret workings of their minds were not hidden from him. He realised clearly enough the ambition on Abelard's behalf which informed them both. Those ambitions could be realised in and through the priesthood alone. What if he could be debarred from the office? Revenge would then be lifelong: it would not consist in one swift, short act. Thinking thus, he formed a subtle plan.

Meanwhile Abelard's own conscience began to be pierced by a sense of shame. He did not regret what had happened so much as the manner of his actions. He had wronged his host, and that treacherously. He determined to make what amends he could, and, with that object in view, he set off for Paris, leaving Heloise behind with his sister.

When he arrived there, he saw Fulbert and offered to make any amends that were possible. There was only one way, said Fulbert, by which amends could be made: he must marry Heloise. Now that, of course, raised the question of clerical celibacy. Abelard was a clerk, and a canon, as was Fulbert. But he was only in minor orders, and he did not hold an executive position in the Church. The Hildebrandine reforms had in this respect tightened matters up a little, but they seem never to have affected in practice those in minor orders. Abelard himself did not regard the marriage of a clerk as in any way unbecoming, provided that he was not in an executive position, that is to say, provided he had not the charge of a parish or a diocese. He regarded celibacy as a law of conduct rather than an ordinance of the faith, and thus as more or less applicable according to circumstances. He had no difficulty in quoting good precedents, and there is no doubt that his view is sound Catholic doctrine. None the less, whilst agreeing to Fulbert's condition of marriage, he asked that it might be kept secret. Fulbert declared that this would satisfy him, and he took leave of Abelard with a kiss of friendship.

But the difficulty of clerical celibacy which Abelard

had anticipated did not form the only or the chief obstacle to his marriage. When he told Heloise what had passed, and bade her prepare for her wedding, he found, to his amazement, that she was inflexibly opposed to any such idea. That it should be suggested at all seemed to appal her, and she argued against it at length, quoting every classical precedent she could think of.

St Paul, by the stark faintness of his praise, had condemned marriage. St Jerome, she reminded him, had quoted Theophrastus on "the intolerable annoyances and perpetual disquietudes" of married life, and had clinched his argument by reminding his readers of Cicero's remark that he could not attend both to philosophy and a wife. She cudgelled her brains for further examples, and in a few moments had quoted from Terence, Jerome, Augustine, Josephus, Pythagoras, and Socrates, all of which sages had pronounced in favour of the incompatibility of marriage and philosophic detachment.

"What concord is there," she asked him, "between pupils and sewing maids, desks and cradles, books or tables and distaffs, pens and spindles? Who, intent upon sacred or philosophic meditation, can endure the wailing of children, the lullabies of the nurses soothing them, the tumultuous mob of the household?"

She went on to quote the classic example of a sage unhappily married, Socrates and his virago of a wife, Xantippe. Did he want her to play the Xantippe to his Socrates? Did he not care if she went down to history as one more example of a woman who had married a great man, and then hindered or ruined his work, by the pressure of her conflicting and irrelevant claims? Did not every precedent show that marriage and philosophy were incompatible? Would it not be "lamentable and indecorous" if he were to dedicate himself, "whom nature has intended for all mankind, to a single woman?" "Nay," she cried, "if thou care not for the prerogative of the clerk, do thou at least defend the dignity of the philosopher."

So she argued, but it was mainly to convince herself and him that reason rather than blind instinct lay behind her fear of marriage. The truth was that she distrusted Fulbert, for she declared that marriage would not lessen the danger of his hostility, and she had no faith whatever in his promises of peace and friendship once "honour was satisfied."

But she did not then urge what was probably her chief reason for this vehement opposition. Later she disclosed it in one of her letters.

> Thou hast not disdained to set forth sundry reasons by which I tried to dissuade thee from our marriage from an ill-starred bed; but wert silent as to many, in which I preferred love to wedlock, freedom to a bond. I call God to witness that if Augustus, ruling over the whole world, were to deem me worthy of the honour of marriage, and to confirm the whole world to me to be ruled by me for ever, dearer to me and of greater dignity would it seem to be called thy mistress than his empress.

"Freedom to a bond"—that was her choice, and she would have freedom. To her marriage was an enchainment not so much upon herself as upon her beloved, and she would have none of it. Neither of

them, she knew well, needed a formal enactment of
their union to ensure fidelity; and if their union was
irregular it was none the less secure. Why, then,
was this abhorrent marriage suggested? It was
simply to satisfy her uncle; and she was convinced that
in spite of all his protestations he was meditating some
vengeance, to which, likely enough, her marriage was
an essential preliminary.

But not even in these voluminous arguments is her
deepest objection to be found. In them she was
seeking to put a rational complexion, such as would
convince her essentially rationalist lover, upon an
inner and overwhelming presentiment. For they are
not even good arguments. She must have known
well enough that in her talk of preferring freedom to
a bond she was proclaiming the common fallacy that
the person without social ties is free. She was using
language to clothe an inner and overwhelming presentiment, and when she found that for all her fluent
argument Abelard was not turned from his purpose,
she at last gave utterance to this pervading intuition.
For, when at last she consented, she said, wringing
her hands and weeping, "One thing remains to the
last, that after the ruin of us both, our suffering may
be no less than the love before it."

Possessed by gloomy forebodings, she left Astrolabe in the care of his aunt, and returned with Abelard
to Paris. When they arrived they were effusively
welcomed by Fulbert. The arrangements were hastily
made. After a very few days they kept a night of
vigil in a church, and next day were quietly and

secretly married there in the presence of Fulbert and a few witnesses.

XI

The insistence upon the necessity of this marriage being kept secret had emanated from Heloise rather than Abelard. There was no end to the ambition she entertained for him, and she knew that her ambitions could only be realised in and through the Church. The Hildebrandine reforms had at least made the marriage of the clergy an absolute bar to the holding of any high office in the Church. If the fact of his marriage had become known officially, he might have been allowed to continue in his mastership at Notre Dame: but, on the other hand, he might not. No one could say for certain what line the Bishop of Paris might take. But at least it was probable that he would be debarred from the teaching of theology.

Accordingly, at her behest, they separated immediately the ceremony had taken place. Abelard went to his old lodgings, and she to her uncle's house. They were never to be together again as man and wife, except for very occasional and fleeting moments.

Time very soon showed Heloise that her intuitive suspicions of her uncle had been just. He, too, had promised to keep the marriage secret. Now he broke the promise. He boasted of it to his friends, and they to others. It was possibly a part of his plan to take his revenge upon Abelard by wrecking his career. Heloise frantically denied it, for she saw all her dreams of Abelard's greatness falling in ruins about her feet. She lied desperately in a vain effort to save the situation. Nobody believed her, and when Fulbert heard what she was doing, he locked her up in her room, and began to ill-treat and to beat her.

Somehow she contrived to get a message to Abelard, and he, for the second time, came to abduct her. But to fly with her was tantamount to admitting the marriage, and that, she still vehemently insisted, was to put an end to any idea of a future career. She would not allow a second elopement. Yet something had to be done; and as she looked at the situation in a calmer light, she saw that to deny the marriage now that she had once more been abducted would be futile. So they evolved a subtle plan whereby, without denying the marriage, Abelard's career might be saved, and her uncle checkmated. It was that she should enter a convent, for that, for all practical purposes, would undo the marriage. She would go to the convent at Argenteuil where she had spent most of her childhood. Only so, they argued, could she be placed out of the reach of her revengeful uncle.

Faced by this crisis, and by the determination of Heloise, Abelard showed the curiously weak indecision which sometimes betrayed him when a time of critical testing came. He gives himself no account of the mental conflict he must have undergone, but merely states the facts as starkly as he can. And the facts are so grim that no man would afterwards wish to dwell on them, or to recall scenes in which he cut so sorry a figure.

The decision made, Abelard took her to Argenteuil, and placed her there in charge of the abbess. When he returned to Paris, and tried to continue his work, he found that he could not banish the sadness of her face. He was sunk in a deep depression; and the wretchedness of his demeanour made the facts plain to all who saw him. He did not deny them, for it was futile. Occasionally, he would ride over to Argenteuil to see Heloise, for, as she was not yet fully professed, the abbess could not prevent her from seeing him. But they were sad visits, for, look and peer as they would, they could see nothing but sadness ahead of them. The one way of escape was the one way that Heloise utterly refused to take. Not all his visits were open, and once at least, as he sadly admitted afterwards, their sorrow and their love overcame them, and did not respect the sanctity of the place in which they were.

Fulbert, meanwhile, seemed to be checkmated. But Heloise, suspicious as she had always been, had not plumbed the black depths of her uncle's hatred. They had, it seemed, escaped his vengeance by the immolation of Heloise. There was nothing now to prevent Abelard's ordination as priest. Yet, perhaps there was a way to make it finally and for ever impossible. There was an old Deuteronomic enactment to debar certain unfortunates from the priesthood, and it was in force in the mediæval Church. Fulbert bethought him of it. Crazy with hatred, he determined to make Abelard as they. He hired some ruffians and gave a heavy bribe to Abelard's servant to

open the door to them. The night came, the hired
ruffians entered Abelard's room as he slept, and,
holding him down, inflicted upon him the most
shameful and terrible of all mutilations. Fulbert's
revenge was complete. Never now could Abelard
hold high office in the Church.

Yet, in spite of it, if Abelard had lost, Fulbert had
not won. For by this act he precisely reversed his
and Abelard's position. Before it, he could with
some justice pose as an injured victim of treachery
and ingratitude, and point to Abelard as the author of
his unhappiness. Whereas Abelard had laid himself
open to the cry that he had brought his misfortunes
upon his own head. But now Fulbert had placed
himself beyond the pale. Mediæval public opinion
could be as ruthless and cruel as Elizabethan opinion
was. But it would not tolerate that. Fulbert immediately forfeited all respect and all pity, while Abelard
gained universal sympathy. Now Fulbert was the
villain of the piece.

Physical pain was the least of the sufferings which
Abelard had now to bear. At first a sense of utter
shame dominated his emotions. He longed to die, or,
if that might not be, to go away alone to some remote
hermitage, where he might never again see a human
face. All Paris was roused to a fury of indignation,
and everyone, from the bishop downwards, rushed
to express to Abelard their abhorrence of the outrage,
and their deep pity for the victim. The crowds
clamoured outside the walls of his house, making the
air hideous with their lamentations. But he wanted

to be quiet, to be alone and undisturbed with his grief and shame. He found this clamant, noisy sympathy inexpressibly distasteful, and commented upon it as not the least of the trials he was condemned to endure.

Then, as he lay there in pain nursing an agony of shame, his mind turned from its thoughts of isolation from humanity as his only way of escape, and fixed itself upon thoughts of revenge. The bishop had promised that the mutilators should be caught and punished. Some of them had in fact been caught, including Abelard's servant, and they had been punished with an insane fury by being made to suffer the same indignity they had inflicted upon their victim, and, in addition, by having their eyes thrust out. In this hideous punishment Abelard had neither part nor lot. He neither sought it nor approved it. But what angered him was that Fulbert was free. It was true that he had had to leave Paris, and that the ecclesiastical authorities impounded the income from his canonry. But he was never punished further, because it could not be proved with utter certainty that he had personally taken any part in the committing of the outrage. Nor was his name removed from the roll of the canons of Notre Dame. He lived on for many years in complete obscurity.

Abelard talked of travelling to Rome, when he was sufficiently recovered, to seek there the justice he seemed to be denied in France. But he had squandered most of his money, and his purse was not sufficiently deep to make any mark upon the endless rapacities of the Curia. An acquaintance, Fulke, Prior of Deuil, eventually persuaded him to give up the idea of appealing to Rome.

But the idea of revenge was not the last of his mental reactions to his sufferings. After all, what was the good of revenge? It could not give him back his lost manhood. As his rancour died away, his suffering led him into deeper thoughts, and he began to show again the greatness that was in him, and which had deserted him during the crisis over his marriage. He was not tempted to curse God and die. Nor did he imagine that God was the author of his misery, though he would have been in perfect accord with much of the thought of his time if he had done so. But, with a mind clarified by suffering, as the mind so often is, he did begin to understand how God can make even the wrath of man, even the hideous violence of a Fulbert, to turn to His praise. There was, after all, he thought, a crude justice in it. He cast his mind back to what had passed so recently—how long ago it seemed?—in the refectory at Argenteuil. The justice might be crude, but it was still justice. So he argued. Fulbert was vile, no doubt, yet "with how just a betrayal had the man repaid me for my former betrayal of him." All his former sins were not sexual. Most of them were traceable to pride. "It occurred to my mind with what glory I had but recently shone, how easily and in a moment this had been brought low, nay, utterly extinguished." And though only blasphemy could discern the finger of God in the crime itself—and of that blasphemy he was never guilty—in the consequences of the crime on his own mind, and in his thought of the future, the presence of God was clear.

The immediate future was also clear. He must give up any idea of ordination to the priesthood, and must say farewell to many of his ambitions. In his new mood of humility that was not very difficult. He could not bring himself to remain in his old position in Paris. Too much water had passed under the bridge for that. Only one way was open to him. He must become a monk, for, in that age, only thus could he gain the requisite freedom from economic necessity to continue his studies, which were now the breath of life to him. He had no vocation to the religious life, and he knew it. But what else could he do? Where else could he find retirement, peace, and an atmosphere of studious calm? Thus he sought, and was granted admission to the famous Abbey of St Denis.

But, first, something had to be decided about Heloise, still immured as a novice in the convent at Argenteuil. Her faithfulness to him was stronger than any strain life could put upon it. She had heard with horror and an agony of grief of her lover's plight, and resolutely agreed to his suggestion, conveyed by a message, that now all was lost, she too should take her vows, and embrace the monastic way of life. Instantly she obeyed; and the more urgently her friends advised her against it, the more resolute was her determination to obey her husband's desire. But she was utterly sad. All her woeful intuitions had been fulfilled, and with a savagery and horror she had not contemplated. Nor had she, and well she knew it, any trace of a vocation. But Abelard desired it, and, for her, that was enough.

Soon, too soon, the day came. Heloise, pale with the weariness of her night of vigil in the chapel, her eyes red with weeping, broke into the famous lamentation of Cornelia:

> Great husband, undeserving of my bed !
> What right had I to bow so lofty a head ?
> Why, impious female, did I marry thee,
> To cause thy hurt ?   Accept the penalty
> That of my own free will I'll undergo.

She entered the chapel.   All the nuns were there.   She advanced to the altar, clothed, as was the custom, in rich and gorgeous robes.   At a sign, she let them fall and stood for a moment naked; and then slowly took the black nun's habit, which the Bishop of Paris blessed and handed to her.   She put it on, and then knelt, publicly reciting her vows.

Let Rémusat, whose pity lends his grave prose lyrical wings, pronounce the epitaph on Heloise, now lost to the world:

> Triste victime, obéissante et non résignée, elle se sacrifiait encore à la volonté et au repos de celui qu'à regret elle avait accepté pour époux, et qu'elle abandonnait en frémissant, pour se donner à l'époux divin sans foi, sans amour, et sans espérance.[1]

XII

Before the story can pass to the next phase in Abelard's life, it is necessary to say something, however

[1] Rémusat, *op. cit.*, vol. i, pp. 69, 70.

briefly, on the question of his purity in the days of his success in Paris, before he loved Heloise, because it has been strongly and bitterly debated in the past by many writers.

It has already been stated that Fulbert readily allowed him to live in his house, and to spend long hours alone with his niece, because he trusted in his reputation for continence, and, further, that this reputation was in his opinion so well founded that he could not at first credit what the scandal-mongers were saying.

All that is in Chapter VI of the *Historia Calamitatum*. But in Chapter V occurs this passage: "It is well known that philosophers, not to say divines, that is to say men intent on the exhortations of Holy Scripture, have laboured principally by the grace of continence. When therefore I was labouring wholly in pride and lechery, the remedy for either malady was by divine grace conferred on me, albeit unwillingly."

But immediately upon the heels of that there follows the statement: "I ever abhorred the uncleanness of harlots, and was withheld from the society of noble women by the assiduity of my studies." It does not finally contradict the first statement, but it does weaken it.

Remembering that Abelard was an abbot when he wrote *Historia Calamitatum*, that he was at the time hiding, in fear for his life, from the extraordinary and savage dissoluteness of his monks, and that his mutilation had naturally warped his views, is it unreasonable to suppose that, when the two statements are taken together, by "labouring wholly in pride and lechery" he meant his association with Heloise, which he described in the ordinary conventional terms of the pulpit oratory of the time? If, as an abbot, he took such a view of the vehemence of his passion for her, he would merely be echoing the common mediæval ideas. The psychological effects of his condition, moreover, would impel him to take such a view of the past. "Labouring wholly in pride and lechery" is, in fact, a rhetorical phrase, and, as such, untrustworthy.

But that is not all the evidence. Fulke, Prior of Deuil, wrote, as has been stated, to dissuade him from going to Rome to prosecute before the Curia his charge against Fulbert. In the letter he accused him of habitual sexual excess. "*Quidquid acquirere poteras in voraginem fornicariæ consumptionis demergere non cessabas.*" That accusation is unsupported by Abelard's bitterest enemies; but that does not necessarily disprove it, though it does weaken it.

Rémusat, concerned for his hero's honour, discounted Fulke's letter on the ground that it wore all the marks of a rhetorical exercise. Lane Poole, whose judgment was cooler and his learning even more profound, in his *Mediæval Thought and Learning*, suggested that the letter was satirical, and that Fulke was merely retailing idle and unfounded rumours, "besides adding not a few from his own gross imagination." [1]

But, on the other hand, the more modern enemies of

---

[1] Reginald Lane Poole, *Studies in Mediæval Thought and Learning* (S.P.C.K.), p. 125, note.

Abelard, notably Cotter Morison, in his *Saint Bernard*, have taken the letter at its face value, asked no questions, and proceeded forthwith to condemnation. Morison quoted Fulke, and then added a sentence so outrageous that not St Bernard himself would have written it: "Pleasure, sensual and animal, was a novelty and a marvel to him. He became suddenly conscious of a fierce fiery thirst for it. He drank deeply, wildly. He then grew fastidious. He required some delicacy of romance, some flavour of emotion, to remove the crudity of his lust. He seduced Heloise." To that outburst he added in a footnote, "Abelard's conduct at the commencement to Heloise was in no wise that of a novice in gallantry but rather such as might have been expected from a hardened offender." [1]

Cotter Morison wrote in 1863; and his heavily righteous condemnations reflect the moral values of his age. But Abelard found a champion in Lane Poole. There was a correspondence, and as a result Lane Poole wrote, "Not long before he died Mr Morison assured me that the view which he had expressed was without foundation."

With the withdrawal of that charge, and the implication involved that Fulke's letter is unreliable, the balance of probability is overwhelmingly in favour of the view that Heloise was Abelard's only love, and his reputation for purity deserved.

[1] Cotter Morison, *Saint Bernard*, p. 263. (Macmillan.)

XIII

The true monastic inspiration had by this time definitely passed into the keeping of the new order of the Cistercians; and their tremendous and brave austerity was a reaction from both the over-luxuriant splendour of Cluny and the spiritual deadness of very many Benedictine houses of religion. But to the Benedictines belonged most of the richer and more famous abbeys. They had few abbeys greater in the world's eyes than that of St Denis, near Paris, to which Abelard now came to seek admission. Founded centuries before by Dagobert, it had been enriched by the frequent gifts of a long line of kings, and was now a royal monastery, regarded as enjoying as by prescriptive right the special favour and protection of the monarchy. To be the abbot of St Denis was to hold one of the greatest positions in the Church in France; and Adam, then the abbot, had so used his office that the prestige of the royal abbey stood higher than ever. But it had ceased to be the home of those who, with true and burning sincerity, had retired from the world to devote themselves to meditation and the contemplative life. Politically, the abbey was of immense importance: spiritually it hàd sunk to a low ebb.

The abbot and his monks none the less took a great pride in their abbey—the same kind of pride that a boy takes in his school, as instinctive and as uncritical. They rejoiced, therefore, when a man with the fame and scholarly prestige of Abelard asked to be admitted. The famous master, by his very presence and by his choice of St Denis of all the abbeys in France, would cast a lustrous mantle over them all.

But it was a broken man who came to them. The natural shame of his bodily injury, together with the bitter sadness and finality of his parting from Heloise, had made him silent and morose. He was in no mood to be fêted; and, to the chagrin of the monks of St Denis, he resolutely declined to play the part of the illustrious convert. A few years ago, he would have delighted in the belief that he was conferring a benefit on so famous an abbey by becoming one of its members. But too much tragedy had come his way since then, and he had suffered far too deeply to be beset any more by such petty conceits.

His immediate purpose was to take his bearings upon life anew, to find some star by which to steer his altered course. For that he needed two things above all else—peace, and the privilege of being alone; and neither boon was granted. At first he showed no desire even to read and study. He answered absent-mindedly when they spoke to him; and he passed his time sunk in silent reflection. But this kind of service was not what the abbot wanted from him. Urged partly, no doubt, by the kindly but unperceiving desire to take him out of himself, but also by the clamour of the monks, he began almost at once to demand that Abelard should charm their ears by his famous lectures, as he had charmed those of his scholars at Notre Dame.

At first he demurred, and pleaded for time. But the abbot's demands were urgent and peremptory. They were reinforced by the daily importunities of his old scholars from Notre Dame, who, deserting that school and its new master, came knocking incessantly at the abbey gates, pleading to be allowed to enter, and to be taught again by their master, as of old. They had a claim which Abelard could never resist. Thus urged, he made an effort to rouse himself from the torpor of his numbness. He reflected sadly that he could no longer play his old part of *Rhinoceros Indomitus*. But he remembered the parable of the Ten Talents, and, under the now strong inspiration of religious conviction, realised that it forcibly applied to himself. "What hitherto I had done from eagerness of wealth or praise, I should study to do now for the love of God, considering that the talent which had been entrusted to me by God would be demanded of me by Him with usury." It was a dangerous mood to indulge in such an abbey as St Denis.

The secret of his previous success as a teacher had chiefly lain in the mutual sympathy always existing between himself and his pupils. Between him and the monks that sympathy did not exist. They expected to be entertained, to be charmed and excited each day by the wit and audacity of which they had heard so much. But now his lecturing did not sparkle. His words betrayed no thrilling antagonisms; and there was a deep earnestness and conviction which had not been conspicuous before. The truth was that he never had the knack of understanding and appealing to older people. The young wandering scholars were not in the least disconcerted or repelled by the changed note of his teaching, for no matter what or how he taught they followed him with an increasing rather than a diminishing devotion to the end of his life. But upon his fellow monks, settled and circumscribed in their mental processes, he exercised no charm whatever. They felt that they were being cheated.

Besides, he was at this time borne upon the crest of the wave of reaction from his former manner of life, and, with perfect sincerity, he was full of the desire to serve God. He had eyes sharp to detect unreality in those who had professed religion, and the unreality of the pretensions of the monks of St Denis was only too obvious. He began to turn his lectures into occasions for the denouncing of the monks for the hypocrisy of their lives. Nothing infuriated him as did hypocrisy; and his fluent and biting tongue did not spare even the abbot.

It was presumption, no doubt, but Abelard was never the man to worry overmuch about that, especially when, as now, he was in the right. His accusations were true; and it was more than time that somebody made them. For the abbey was altogether too royal. As St Bernard said, "It served Cæsar rather than God," and the abbot relied on the political prestige of his position to deter and silence any criticism which might be made. The Rule was relaxed, and both abbot and monks were abandoned to the secular life and the habitual breaking of their vows. Not even the vow of chastity was observed. Abelard's accusations of "dissoluteness and notorious infamy" are amply supported by the letters of St Bernard and by the annals of the abbey itself. Not a hundred years had passed since the same disorder had brought upon them a compulsory reformation at the hand of St Odilo.

Adam, the abbot, had no intention of entertaining another Odilo. Yet he could not silence Abelard, for, having once been persuaded to break his silence, he perversely refused to be quiet. He detected unreality; and he was determined to rebuke it. He firmly continued to do so. The monks were furious, and Adam was troubled, for he could hardly treat Abelard as though he were the ordinary young novice. Nor could he take severe disciplinary measures, for many eyes were fixed upon the abbey as a consequence of the distinguished novice it harboured. He puzzled over the problem until, at last, light came. There would clearly be no peace until the abbey was rid of this embarrassing and all too eloquent voice. He could hardly silence its owner by an over-arbitrary exercise of authority. But could he not make use of the unceasing clamours of the scholars outside the gates, and so get rid of him? He sent for Abelard, and, employing all the arts of persuasion, he managed to convince him that his duty lay with his old scholars. He must use his gifts to train them for God's service. But that he could not do whilst still in the abbey; so it would be best for him to go to Maisoncelle, in the province of Champagne, and there found a priory for them, which should be under the nominal direction of the abbot. Abelard's spirits had revived a little; and he had shaken off his torpor in the heat of his indignation. He saw that he would do no good by remaining at St Denis; and the abbot's suggestion coincided very much with his own inclinations. He agreed, and left St Denis in 1120, being then forty-one years old.

The Champagne roads and lanes were soon dotted with the trudging figures of the wandering scholars. Abelard was a magnet who could draw them away from the gaiety and roistering of Paris and Orleans, and the comparative comfort of their lodgings there. Maisoncelle was no more than an isolated hermitage, but his name was sufficient to lure them into any desert or wilderness. Wherever Abelard was, there was his school. Very soon he had a multitude of followers. The chronicles put their number at 3000. It is not surprising, for to his already tremendous reputation was now added the embarrassing fame naturally attaching to the hero of the street-singers' ballads.

Maisoncelle soon became so crowded that other masters began to complain that Abelard was emptying their schools. They gave vent to their woes and their jealousy in a manner strangely redolent of the modern industrialist when beset by the competition which in theory he regards as the foundation of all virtue. They did not object to competition as such, they said, but this particular competition was unfair. They complained that Abelard was trading upon his recent notoriety; that he was guilty of unprofessional conduct; that to set up a school in opposition to theirs was not consonant with his newly taken vows to follow the professed life of religion. He was a monk now, not a master, and his proper place was within the walls of his monastery. Thus complaining, they looked round for some more concrete accusation, whereby they might denounce him to the authorities, and have him officially silenced. They very soon found what they wanted in the general tenor of his teaching, which, since his Paris days, had undergone a remarkable and a fruitful change.

XIV

Abelard was not as forgetful of his vows as his critics strove to persuade themselves. The crisis through which he had passed had hardly brought him a real vocation for the monastic life; but it had certainly changed the direction in which his mind was moving. All things had been previously seen in the perspective of self. But now God rather than himself was the ever-present reality. It was idle for him to deny that he had a great talent for teaching, and, meditating upon the parable of the Ten Talents, he had determined to dedicate his gifts to the service of God and His Church. But as to the precise manner in which his gifts, thus dedicated, were to be used he must judge for himself. He would bow to the

Church up to a point, but he would maintain his own ways before her, and serve her in his own way and at his own time.

The immediate question he had to answer was: What was the kind of service, of which the Church then had need, which could be rendered most fruitfully by a man of his particular capacities? In his old controversy in the school of Anselm at Laon he found the answer. At Laon he had provoked the wrath of his fellows by suggesting that there was no real separation between secular and religious knowledge. All knowledge was one. It was absurd to suggest, as it was suggested, that "scientific reading is improper for any religious person." Science and Religion go hand in hand. Both are rungs in the ladder which leads the believer to the Reality that is God. So it is, he argued, with literature. Many of his lectures were devoted to showing that the more eloquent and persuasive of the Apostles and Fathers "exhibited greater graces in his teaching as he possessed a more extensive knowledge of literature before it." The study of the great secular and classical literature is therefore, he concluded, "specially recommended by Divine direction."

It was, then, his aim to achieve a synthesis of knowledge, to show that each of the so-called secular branches of learning had a definite and vital contribution to make to the well-being of the crown and glory of them all, theology. For that theology was the goal and the crown of all knowledge he was now convinced.

To modern ears it sounds an optimistic programme.

But in the first half of the twelfth century it was still possible for a single mind to make itself acquainted with, if not to master, all the direct knowledge available. And, though ambitious, it was needed. The separation between religious and secular knowledge, the assumption of a necessary and fixed antagonism between them, which sounds so strange to us, was in that day very widely held. The authority of the whole Church was striving to keep its members unspotted from the classics, and though they were studied, more or less secretly, in every monastery and convent, and though every contemporary writer of merit, not excepting St Bernard himself, betrayed his debt to them in every page he wrote, their sweetness was that of stolen fruit. To suggest that it would be well to apply the fruits of learning and the sense of proportion gleaned from that impious field to the elucidation of Holy Scripture was an audacity few would have ventured. In the orthodox view of things, Ovid was beyond the pale, and Virgil, though secretly regretted by half the zealots of the Church, who had resolutely put him behind them, was a snare and a delusion.

Abelard's aim at Maisoncelle was to shed upon the obscurities of Holy Scripture and theology the light of literary proficiency. "Giving my attention principally to Holy Scripture, I did not altogether lay aside the teaching of the secular arts in which I was more fully versed, and which they demanded most of me; but made them as it were a hook wherewith I might draw them, enticed by the philosophic savour, to a study of the true philosophy as was the custom of the greatest

of the Christian philosophers, Origen." There was now
more than one parallel between himself and Origen;
and he viewed himself as Origen's natural heir.

His lectures in the new manner attracted attention
far and wide, much to the chagrin of those masters
whose schools he was emptying. But it was easy now
for his opponents to hurl their accusations, for he
himself had provided them with ammunition. In his
exaltation of secular philosophy to the position of a
handmaid of religion, he was flirting with distinct
unorthodoxy, if not actually with heresy. They even
accused him of a kind of necromantic familiarity with
sinful knowledge. But that accusation was too wild
to be of much help to them, and he had no difficulty
in showing the inherent stupidity of the mind which
could bring such a charge.

> No scientific reading is improper for any religious
> person. . . . No one can call any science evil, though it
> be itself concerned with evil, which an upright man
> requires. Guilt consists not in the knowledge of a sin,
> but in its commission. But if any knowledge were sinful,
> then were it sinful to know certain things. So then God,
> who knoweth all things, could not be held guiltless of sin.
> For in Him alone is the fullness of all knowledge, whose
> gift all knowledge is.

His enemies could not answer. But obscurantists are
never mollified by the bare act of proving that their
arguments are based on faulty premises. They are
only the more infuriated, and look about for some
other cause of offence.

Abelard had only been a few months in Maisoncelle; and he was again involved in a conflict. It

was not of his seeking, but he could never refuse a battle; and it had this good effect that it banished the last vestiges of his morose torpor, and renewed his vitality. Life was worth living again. Both he and his pupils hurled themselves into the fray all the more vigorously because they were now convinced that this was a holy controversy.

The vivid imagery of his lectures was reinforced by a steady stream of writings, all conceived in the suspect Origen vein. In them his momentarily checked enemies found all they needed.

In his theological lectures he had been making some dangerous remarks. "How far are they worthy of attention who assert that faith is not to be built up or defended by reasoning?" Considering that no less influential a churchman than St Bernard spent a large part of his time asserting that very thing, to ask such a question was, to say the least, injudicious. Most of his teaching turned upon the same point, for he was now launching himself in his true, his historically important *métier* of the Catholic Rationalist. He had questioned the old Ransom theory of the Atonement. He was full of analogies and explanations of the mystery of the Holy Trinity. He wrote the *Sic et Non* to provide a rationale for the readier interpretation of the Scriptures. In this book he stated the difficulties of biblical and doctrinal interpretation with embarrassing frankness by setting on opposite sides of the same page contradictory texts and sentences from the Bible and the Fathers. Then he stated the principles by which such apparent contradictions and difficulties might be reconciled. The reader must be wary of placing too ardently literal an interpretation upon apocryphal books or sayings: he must recognise that one word might have more than one meaning, particularly when used by different authors: he must realise that not even apostles and prophets are infallible: and he must remember that, so far as the Fathers are concerned, they sometimes retracted their earlier views, and they often quoted other people's opinions without either endorsing or condemning them. Having given heed to all this counsel, and applied it so far as he was able, the reader must balance in his own mind the difficulties of interpretation still remaining, and take his stand with what seems to him to be the better side. Abelard was perfectly explicit on the point that Holy Scripture does not err in itself. But he pointed out that undoubted difficulties none the less exist, and that no theory of inspiration could remove manifest contradictions. He suggested that the reader must account for his bewilderment either by postulating a faulty manuscript, or by admitting his insufficient grasp of heavenly wisdom. The authority of the Fathers was less absolute, and the reader was informed that he might, without loss of fidelity, differ from them if he wished.

It was not heresy: but it was most inflammable. As though realising his danger, he declared that he would add a solution of the problems he had raised. But he neglected to do it; and so was accused of merely seeking occasion for scandal. The accusation was unjust; but it was not unnatural.

But the *Sic et Non* had a limited scope. He had written it at a great pace, and no sooner was it finished than he turned his attention to another part of the theological field. "I composed a certain tractate of theology, *of Unity in the Holy Trinity*, for our scholars . . . which tractate indeed, when numbers had seen and read it, began generally to please its readers because it appeared to satisfy all alike upon these questions."

That it "satisfied all alike" is hardly an accurate statement of fact. There were many whom it did not satisfy at all (except in so far as they sought occasion to silence him), and who saw in his attempts to bring reason to the elucidation of the divine mystery of the Trinity, nothing but the seeds of a particularly damnable and dangerous heresy. That his book had a sensational success only made it the more suspect in the eyes of his enemies. The masters whose schools he had emptied saw their chance. They copied the more startling passages, without any qualifying contexts, and sent them to such Church authorities as had fallen foul of Abelard in the past. They challenged him in their schools, charging him with applying the methods of dialectic to theology—which was exactly what the *Sic et Non* had done—and of casting over Holy Scripture the false glamour of profane science. Abelard seems not to have believed that they would dare actually to engage themselves in open conflict with a dialectician of his fame. He taunted them. "It is a case of the well-known fable of the fox disdaining the grapes he cannot reach. Similarly, modern doctors, being unable to understand dialectic, call it deception. To them, all they cannot understand is madness, all that passes them by, a delusion."

Events now moved swiftly towards a crisis, and it became evident that a trial of strength could not be avoided. The opposing forces began to line up, and to estimate their strength. Three chief figures emerged from the ranks of Abelard's enemies, and they led the attack on him. With all of them he had quarrelled before.

The first was Roscelin. He had by now been admitted to favour again, and was a canon of St Martin at Tours. In the introduction to the second part of his theological tractate, Abelard had castigated several heretical propositions on the Trinity. He did not name their authors, but some of them were certainly aimed at Roscelin's head. The book came into Roscelin's hand. He had always been proud and fiery tempered, and the hardships and disgrace he had had to face had made him rancorous. Moreover, though he had been officially reconciled to the Church, a faint odour of suspicion still clung about his name. He was perpetually looking for an opportunity of demonstrating his complete orthodoxy, and Abelard's book seemed to him to afford the chance he needed. At one blow he could demonstrate his own innocence, and pay off some old scores into the bargain. He did not defend himself against the charges Abelard had made, but treated them as though they were too ridiculous to be worth refuting. But instead he denounced Abelard to the authorities, writing to the

Bishop of Paris to demand Abelard's heretical head on a charger. Soon Abelard heard of it, and, in the heat of his annoyance, promptly wrote a furious letter to the Bishop of Paris, declaiming against Roscelin as the "old enemy of the Catholic faith," whose heresies had already been condemned by the Council of Soissons. So strong was his belief in his own complete orthodoxy that he did not imagine that the same condemnation awaited him.

His other enemies had less notoriety than Roscelin, but more power. They were the two students of whom he had fallen foul at Laon, Alberic of Rheims, and Lotulph of Novara. Both of them were now masters of schools in Rheims, and Alberic was a personage of great and rising importance in the Church. He was Prior of St Sixte, Archdeacon of Rheims, and, what in that day was far more important, he was the protégé of St Bernard, who had tried to persuade Pope Honorius II to appoint him to the bishopric of Chalons on the death of William of Champeau. Upon this Alberic the brunt of the conflict fell, and he showed himself a resourceful antagonist, well versed in all the arts of intrigue.

These men, actuated by their various motives, now set themselves to break Abelard. Roscelin saw that by Abelard's fall he himself might regain the unhesitating regard of the Church. Alberic and Lotulph, worthier opponents, for whom Abelard himself had no word of scorn, fought because they pictured themselves as the intellectual successors of Anselm and

William of Champeau in the holy war against Nominalism, and they thought that in crushing Abelard they
would deal a grievous blow at the whole nominalist
position. The fact that Abelard was not technically
a nominalist does not seem to have struck them.
But whatever he was, he was certainly no realist,
and perhaps that was enough. They were convinced,
too, that his exaltation of reason and the secular
studies constituted a serious challenge and danger to
Christendom, as exemplified in the Church.

On Abelard's side of the controversy there was only
himself and his scholars, and in a trial such as this
was to be they could be of little help. One bishop, it
is true, the famous Geoffrey of Chartres, covertly
sympathised with his teaching and his intellectual
position, but the part he was to play in Abelard's
defence was almost exactly paralleled, both in its
strength and its weakness, by the famous speech to the
Sanhedrin of Gamaliel as it is reported in the fifth
chapter of the book of the *Acts of the Apostles.*

The two sides represented a clash of ideas, and on its
issue the freedom of thought hung. They prepared
the ground by denouncing each other, whilst they
sought some occasion that might bring matters to a
head. Alberic found it. He went to Radulphus,
Archbishop of Rheims, and persuaded him to consult with Conan, Bishop of Palestrina and Papal Legate
in France. The two prelates met, and decided to
call together a Council to meet at Soissons. They
summoned Abelard to it, and ordered him to bring
with him his book of theology. It was less than twelve

months since he had been tactfully dismissed from the abbey of St Denis, and sent to Maisoncelle.

XV

The Council met in 1121 at Soissons, the town in which Roscelin had previously suffered his own condemnation. (It does not appear that Roscelin was present at this Council: the irony of history did not extend so far.) The town was within the metropolitan jurisdiction of Rheims, and the Archbishop had summoned his suffragan bishops, Alberic and Lotulph, various masters of schools, and Geoffrey, Bishop of Chartres.

When Abelard arrived in obedience to his summons, he found that Alberic and his friends had already been busy. They had been preaching to the citizens, and striving, with some success, to create the kind of atmosphere which would make Abelard's acquittal a matter of difficulty on account of its unpopularity. When Abelard and his following of young scholars rode into the town they found that they were execrated by the people, who had been told by Alberic that he had both preached and written the abominable heresy that there were three Gods, and not one. The feeling was bitter against them, and they narrowly escaped being stoned—an episode which shows how universally detested was the crime of heresy in mediæval Europe.

Abelard detested heresy no less bitterly than did

the people of Soissons, or the prelates sitting on the Council. He could conceive no label more degrading; and he was certain that he had neither said nor written anything that amounted to it. Had he not begun his disputed book by explicitly stating that the entire foundation of all that is good rests solely upon faith in the Holy Trinity? It was true that he had sought to establish that faith by the use of human reason. But he had done so to defend it against "those philosophers and heretics who vaunt themselves in opposing every creed by human rationalism." He was not trying to propagate heresy, but to defeat it by turning the heretic's weapons to his own confusion, for which there was a respectable precedent in Anselm's dealings with Roscelin. And, in face of his precise statement in the book of his intention only to put forward "that which is probable, agreeable to human reason, and not opposed to religious belief," it was hard to see how any reasonable man could find in the book material on which to base so damaging a charge as that of heresy. Otto of Friesingen, reviewing the proceedings in his History, cautiously suggested that the effect of some of Abelard's statements might be to efface the distinction between the different members of the Trinity. But, if that was so, the point was never made at the Council.

Immediately he arrived at Soissons, he sought out the Papal Legate, delivered the book to him, and declared himself ready to make correction or to give satisfaction if it could be shown that he had written anything contrary to the Catholic Faith. He was merely repeating a promise already made in the book itself. In this proffered submission to authority, his motive was rather loyalty to the Church than fear of punishment. From the beginning of his life to the end of it Abelard did not cease to regard himself as a good churchman.

His confidence in his own orthodoxy was not unjustified, for the Council found it extremely difficult to wring out of the book any precise charge. Day by day its members met. Except for the Bishop of Chartres, all of them were actuated by the common desire to find that in the book which would justify them before the eyes of the world in condemning both it and its author. But not even the anger-sharpened eyes of Alberic could find passages sufficiently offensive. Time slowly passed. Days turned into weeks, and still Abelard had not been summoned before the members of the Council to account for his words. Slightly embarrassed, they were still closeted with the book.

Whilst waiting for a summons or some decision, Abelard busied himself in preaching to the clergy and people of the town expounding his opinions, and showing that in them there was nothing inconsistent with the Catholic Faith. By his gifts of oratory and persuasion he persuaded them with little difficulty that Alberic's crude charges were baseless. Those who had begun by shouting insults in the streets and trying to stone him were now asking the reason of all this delay. They suggested that perhaps the Council was seeking a graceful way of escape from a false position.

"Lo," they said, "now he speaks in public; and no

one says one word in answer. The Council is coming rapidly to an end, that was convened chiefly, as we have been told, to condemn him. Can it be that his judges have recognised that they rather than he are in error?"

His accusers felt that if they delayed any longer, the delay would be tantamount to an acquittal. Alberic found that councils were dilatory bodies, and he therefore decided to force matters to a head.

In so doing he made his one false move, for he determined to beard *Rhinoceros Indomitus* in his den, and to trap him into an admission so damaging that the Council would have something definite upon which to condemn him. His experiences at Laon should have taught him a greater discretion and a truer estimate of his powers. He was merely made to look ridiculous.

Taking some of his friends with him to act as witnesses he visited Abelard in his lodgings. He tried to disarm him, to put him off his guard, by the blandness of his manner. He put on the manner of a friendly, unofficial visit, and discussed the weather, and politics, and for some time kept the talk clear of religion. But then, as small talk languished, Alberic, in a tone of elaborate unconcern, as though it were not after all of any great consequence, asked him why it was that he had denied that God had begotten Himself, when all men knew that God was One, and that God begat God.

Abelard was not at all deceived. He replied sharply, "On this point, if you wish it, I will reason."

"We pay no heed to human reason," replied

Alberic. He knew Abelard's powers of argument. "Nor," he added, "do we pay heed even to the evidence of our senses in such matters, but only to the words of authority."

"Turn the page of the book and you will find the authority."

Alberic had brought a copy. As he fumbled, Abelard seized it from him, and turned the pages over until he found the place. He then thrust it at his enemy, showing him a quotation from no less an authority than St Augustine, "Whoso supposes God to be so powerful as Himself to have begotten Himself errs the more greatly in that not only God is not so, but no 'creature,' either spiritual or corporeal. For there is nothing whatsoever that may beget itself."

Abelard's followers laughed, while Alberic's blushed at his discomfiture. Alberic said hastily, "It is well that it should be clearly understood."

It was bluster and it deceived no one, least of all Abelard, who proceeded to turn the tables upon Alberic by saying blandly, "It is nothing new, and of little importance at present, since you required of me the words only and not the sense. But if you want the sense of them explained to you, I am quite ready to do it, and I will show you that you have yourself fallen into that heresy by which the Father is made to be his own Son."

Alberic then took refuge in threats that neither the power of reason, nor even the authority of St Augustine himself, would now avail to save him, and flung himself out of the room in a rage.

He had not trapped Abelard, nor enticed him into any damaging admission. He had merely been made to look foolish in front of his own followers. Nor had he anything to report to the Council upon which it was possible to take action. The members began to fear that their deliberations would be vain, and they would be made a laughing-stock. Alberic's popularity began to wane; and the most considerable person at the Council, the Bishop of Chartres, seemed unaccountably to be ranging himself on the opposite side. Still nothing was done. It seemed to Alberic to be high time to try other methods.

It came at last to the final day of the sitting of the Council. Some decision had to be made. The members sat and listened listlessly to the Archbishop and the Papal Legate interminably discussing what might be done with this man who ought to be checked, but against whom no proper charge could be brought. The discussion droned on; but still they seemed as far away as ever from a decision. Then, as though from sheer inanition, the talk ceased, and the members sat in perplexed silence, until, at last, the Bishop of Chartres rose and said:

All of you, Sirs, that are here present know that this man's teaching, whatsoever it be, and his intellect have had many supporters and followers in whatsoever he has studied, that he has greatly diminished the fame of his own masters, as of ours, and that, so to speak, his vine has spread its branches from sea to sea. If, as I do not think, you condemn him by prejudice, even rightly, you must know that you will offend many, and there will not be wanting those who will wish to defend him; especially as in the writing here present we see nothing which may deserve any open calumny. . . . Take heed lest you confer more renown upon him by violent action. But if you are disposed to act canonically against him, let his doctrine or his writing be brought into our midst, and let him be questioned and allowed freely to reply, that convicted or confessing his error, he be henceforward silent.

But that counsel was altogether too diplomatic for Alberic and his friends. They replied at once with sarcastic emphasis, "O wise counsel, that we should contend against his verbosity whose arguments or sophisms the entire world could not withstand."

The Bishop of Chartres was still determined to avoid taking any action, if he could prevail, for he knew that any formal condemnation would be unjust, and he suspected that it would also be futile in practice. Could not the onus of making a decision be shifted to other shoulders? He made a new suggestion. There were, he said, too few present to discuss so weighty a matter. The case needed a more thorough examination than could then be given it. Why not send Abelard back to the Abbey of St Denis? His abbot was present with them. Let him recall him, and keep him within the abbey until his case could be adequately dealt with.

To this course the Legate agreed. He prorogued the sitting and went to say Mass before the decision should be announced.

But during the interval Alberic and Lotulph, absenting themselves from Mass, disconcertedly consulted together as to how they might prevent the

Bishop's proposal from taking effect. The last thing they wanted was that Abelard should be tried by a council sitting in a diocese in which they had no authority, and to which they would not be summoned. The Abbey of St Denis was outside the jurisdiction of the Archbishop of Rheims. They went to the Archbishop, and spoke of their fears to him. They persuaded him that it would be taken as a slight upon himself if at this stage Abelard was sent back to the diocese of Paris. They had no great difficulty in prevailing upon his pride.

Immediately the Legate re-entered the room after the interval they hastened to him, and, telling him of the dissatisfaction of the Archbishop, persuaded him also to change his mind. He was not so easily persuaded as the Archbishop had been, but eventually he none the less agreed to what they proposed. It was that Abelard's book was to be condemned without further inquiry, then publicly burnt, and that he himself was to be sentenced to perpetual enclosure in some strange monastery.

"If you want a due and proper reason for condemning the book," they urged, "it should be sufficient that he has read it publicly, and lent it to many, in spite of the fact that it has not received the *imprimatur* of the Church." Then, unctuously, "It will be a good example against similar presumption in others."

The Bishop of Chartres, overhearing what was being arranged, slipped out in search of Abelard, who was waiting not far away. He told him about it, and said

that as he saw no way of preventing it, the best thing
he could do was to suffer it as quietly as he could, for
he could not save him against the unshakable will of
the majority. But if he bore himself meekly all
would yet be well, for the violence and the injustice
were too openly outrageous. Public opinion would
save him. And once the Papal Legate had left
Soissons, and was free of the influence of the Archbishop of Rheims, he would be certain to revoke his
judgment, as soon as he saw its wide unpopularity,
and release him from confinement.

Then Abelard was summoned. It was the first time
he had appeared before his judges. He saw, as he
entered, that a fire was already kindled, and that he
was not allowed to urge one word in his own defence.
They told him coldly to throw his book into the fire.
In silence, he and they watched it burn until only a
heap of black ash was left. Then a voice was heard
drowsily murmuring, "was it not written in the book
that God the Father alone is almighty?"

The Legate turned angrily on the speaker, saying,
"When our common Faith holds and professes that
there are three Almighties, it is hardly to be believed
that a little child would so err."

An old master of Abelard's, Tirric of Chartres, was
present. He laughed gently, and began to quote,
". . . Yet there are not three Almighties but one
Almighty."

The Bishop of Chartres, who had been forced
miserably to watch what he knew to be unjust and yet
could not prevent, then took fire. He, too, quoted—

from *Daniel*. "'Thus, ye foolish children of Israel, neither judging nor knowing the truth, ye have condemned the daughter of Israel. Return to judgment,' and judge the judge himself, ye who have set up such a judge for the instruction of the Faith and the correc-. tion of error: who when he ought to judge out of his own mouth hath condemned himself. This day, by divine mercy, deliver him who is plainly innocent like Susannah of old."

Tirric was rebuked; but the appeal for justice came too late. The Book had already been burned, and now the Archbishop rose to pronounce judgment. As he did so, he turned towards the Bishop of Chartres, and said, "Verily, sir, the Father is almighty, the Son is almighty, and the Holy Ghost is almighty, and whoso dissenteth from this is evidently in error, nor is he to be heard. And yet, if it please thee, it is well that this our brother expound his faith before us all, that it be either approved or disapproved, as may be fitting."

It was a merely formal invitation. But Abelard, thinking that at last he was to be allowed to defend himself, began to speak. But there was yet another humiliation, the cruellest. He was immediately interrupted, and coldly told that he was not there to make professions of his own. All that he was required to do was to recite the Athanasian Creed, "and lest thou dost not know it, read it from this written copy." They handed him the copy. It was a studied insult, hurled by ungenerous men at an enemy greater than they, who had been given no chance of speaking in his own defence. His feelings choked him, but he stammered and stumbled through it as best he could. He was then formally committed to the custody of the Abbot of St Médard, and the Council of Soissons was dissolved.

XVI

Within less than two years Abelard had suffered two great shocks, the one in his body and the other in his mind. But whereas the pain of the mutilation had given to him faith rather than caused him to lose it, now his anguish was such that he echoed again and again in mechanical repetition St Anthony's complaint, "Good Jesus, where wert thou?" "To the former I had come by my own fault. But to this so open a violence, a sincere intent and love of our Faith had brought me which compelled me to write."

Geoffrey, Abbot of St Médard, and his monks, received their prisoner with kindness and consideration. He had been sentenced to what was virtually imprisonment, but he was allowed to wander at will in the neighbourhood of the monastery. But kindness could not greatly lighten his burden. He had been condemned as a heretic by an outrageous decree, when his only desire had been to serve the Church. No amount of courtesy or consideration could alter the fact of his branding. As he walked, he brooded continually over the injustice, and was wretchedly unhappy.

Then, one day, wandering aimlessly, he suddenly met another old adversary of his, Gosvin of Douai, who had challenged him to debate in the old days at Paris which now seemed so far away. He was now a monk of the monastery of St Crépin, not very far away from St Médard. The story of their meeting is not mentioned by Abelard, but it is told in the *Life of St Gosvin*.

When they met Gosvin decided to treat him in the spirit of sweet and sanctimonious forgiveness. He talked to him, mingling consolation, advice, and instruction, preaching patience and modesty, and suggesting that he was not so much imprisoned as released from worldly honour and temptation. He had only to practise honesty and all would be well. This was too much. Abelard felt that this volley of sententiousness savoured of rather more than charity. At first he had been surprisingly silent, but, at the word Honesty, he burst violently into speech. "Honesty! Why do you preach and boast of honesty to me? There are many who prate of all kinds of honesty, but have not sufficient knowledge to answer the simple question, What is Honesty?"

"Yes, you are indeed right," replied Gosvin angrily. "Many who presume to lecture on the different types of honesty entirely ignore the thing itself. And if henceforward you say or hazard anything that may imply that I am lessening the claims of honesty or sincerity, you will have to reckon with us, and you will then find that we are not ignorant of honesty when you see us pursuing your deceit." The writer goes on ingenuously to describe the extreme terror of *Rhinoceros Indomitus*.

But it was little more than an incident within an episode, though this slanging match did have the effect of shaking Abelard's lethargy a little. Very soon, however, his imprisonment at St Médard came to an abrupt end. Things fell out as the Bishop of Chartres had said they would. The unrelenting intrigues of Alberic had defeated their own object by the violence with which they were pursued. The Papal Legate, once outside the diocese of Rheims, ordered Abelard to be released, and to be sent back to his own abbey. He blamed the jealousy of the clergy of Rheims for what had happened, and most of the other members of the Council hastened to disavow their share in its proceedings. The really monstrous injustice had raised him high in popular favour again, and in any case the whole procedure was of thoroughly doubtful validity by Canon Law, for Abelard, being technically a monk of St Denis, it did not lie within the competence of any council or synod called by the Archbishop of Rheims to condemn him.

But, be that as it may, the fact remained that the slur of heresy had been cast, which, in those days, was no laughing matter. He was still and with good reason gloomy and morose when the embarrassed Abbot of St Denis received him back again.

XVII

They killed no fatted calf at the Abbey of St Denis to greet Abelard's return. Neither the habits nor the

personnel of the monks had changed since he had left
them at the abbot's request, and during his absence
they had been restfully free from zealous but tiresome
attempts to change the manner of their lives. But
his absence had not been long, and they remembered
all too vividly the sharpness of his tongue as he
lashed their insincerities and their vices. Suspicion
and hostility greeted him when he returned, and none
of the brothers extended any welcome to him.

He had little to hope for. The decrees of the
Council of Soissons might have been half disavowed,
but no amends had been made to the victim of their
injustice, and though, with his change of abbeys, the
perpetual imprisonment was no longer called by that
name, his present situation none the less approximated to it, except that in being removed from St
Médard to St Denis he had made a change for the
worse. At St Médard he had at least received con-
siderate treatment.

No sooner had he returned than the abbot sent for
him and demanded that he should again lecture to the
monks. He had hoped to be left in peace, a desire
which was his invariable reaction to sore unhappiness,
but he bowed to authority and did as he was bidden.
His troubles at Soissons had either cowed him or
taught him an unwonted discretion, for he no longer
attempted to reprove his hearers for the shortcomings
of their lives. So far was he from that that he made
a real effort to avoid anything which was contro-
versial, and, robbed of much of their salt, his lectures
were listlessly delivered.

But it made little difference, for in a few months he was once more in trouble. It was not of his seeking, and it arose quite inadvertently. To speak plainly, it was as purely silly a storm in a teacup as can be imagined, but it earned him a severe flogging, and led at last to his precipitate flight. The whole question was nothing more important than the possibility that Dionysius the Areopagite had been Bishop not of Athens, as the tradition asserted, but of Corinth.

It happened that as he was lecturing one day, the Venerable Bede's exposition of the *Acts of the Apostles* came under discussion. The commentary had reached Chapter XVII, which describes St Paul at Athens, and his comparative lack of success there. "But certain men clave unto him and believed: among whom was Dionysius the Areopagite." Now this Dionysius had traditionally become Bishop of Athens, and, as St Denis, was the patron saint of France and of the abbey called by his name. Bede had asserted that he became Bishop of Corinth and not of Athens.

Abelard casually and innocently mentioned Bede's assertion. Unwittingly he had flicked a sore nerve, and he was immediately surrounded by a ring of clamorous and infuriated brethren. For, though he did not know it, the question had arisen before, and the then abbot, Hilduin, had made a special journey to Greece to settle the matter. Having travelled far and studied deep, Hilduin had written a volume of immense learning, proving beyond all possible doubt that St Denis of France and Dionysius, Bishop of Athens, were one and the same. If Bede had had the temerity to deny it, then "Bede was a most mendacious writer"; and if, as Abelard mildly suggested, Bede's authority, "whose writings the entire body of Latin Churches consult," was better than Hilduin's, then Abelard was not only a detractor of the fame of the abbey, he was nothing less than a traitor to the king of France. Disconcerted by this sudden fury, he suggested that after all it was not a very great matter whether St Denis had presided over the Sees of Athens or Corinth, "since he had won so bright a crown before God."

It was a soft answer, and, for Abelard, extraordinarily tactful, but it turned aside no wrath. It rather fanned the flames. The abbot was informed, a full chapter was called, the offender was solemnly and ceremoniously denounced, threatened with the royal displeasure, and violently whipped. The question of the identity of St Denis had turned out to be serious enough for him.

To realise that both the monks and Bede were wrong comes near to turning the episode into farce. Yet so it is. Dionysius the Areopagite was Bishop of Athens, wherein Bede erred; but he was not St Denis of France. The French patron Saint was Dionysius, Bishop of Corinth.

XVIII

Faced, as he now was, by a suspicion and enmity plainly implacable, Abelard's nerve failed. He waited his opportunity, and, when one night it came, he scaled the abbey wall in the darkness. Travelling fast throughout all that night, and the next day, he made his way to Provins, where Count Theobald dwelled. He cast himself under his powerful protection, and the Count, listening to the recital of his woes with sympathy, granted him permission to live as a hermit in a cell near Troyes, under the direction of the Prior of Troyes, who was an old and mutual friend to them both.

But, as before, flight could only raise difficulties: by itself, it could settle nothing. By his flight Abelard had placed himself in the position of an absconding monk, in the Middle Ages a serious position to be in. And in his case it was the more serious in that he was still officially lying under the ban of the Council of Soissons, still officially imprisoned in St Denis. The arm of the Church was long, and against it Count Theobald, powerful feudal nobleman though he was, could hardly prove an adequate protection. Realising this, Abelard wrote a letter to the Abbot of St Denis, asking for reconciliation, and for formal permission to lead the monastic life in a hermit's cell under the direction of the Prior of Troyes. In his letter he suggested that Bede might have been deceived in the matter of the Areopagite, or that perhaps there had been more than one Dionysius. It was useless: his plea was angrily rejected.

For both the abbot and the monks of St Denis felt that with the defection of Abelard a certain distinction had been withdrawn. Whilst he was with them, they did all they could to make his life wretched, and they rejoiced when their persecution drove him away. But no sooner had he left them than they wanted him to return, regarding his absence as a slur cast upon their good name. They could not make up their minds. Pride in their house urged them to seek the glory of his fame; self-indulgence led them to drive away the sadness and accusation of his presence. For these reasons the abbot had rejected his request, but immediately he had done so he made some excuse to visit Count Theobald. Abelard heard of this projected visit, and immediately went himself to the Count to ask his good offices to persuade the abbot to allow him to live monastically in some suitable place other than within the walls of St Denis. The Count did what he could, but he was not strong enough to protect him against the Abbot of St Denis, who refused his plea no less decisively than before. He did more. He threatened Abelard with excommunication if he did not at once return, and included the Prior of Troyes in the ban if he should presume to shelter him.

Excommunication was an irresistible weapon, for it occurred to very few to defy it. Abelard was not one of them. As he was starting on his journey, however, the news came of the abbot's sudden death whilst travelling home from Provins. At once he changed his direction and went to Meux to appeal to the bishop. But the bishop was no less obdurate. He, too, rejected the plea. Abelard had now but one card left to play—an appeal to the king himself, Louis VI. Trembling and apprehensive, he played it —and won. The king's steward called the parties to the dispute together, and, having heard both sides, took the admirably common sensible view that the monks, by seeking to retain Abelard against his will, "might easily incur scandal and could gain nothing, since my way of life and theirs could in no way be made to agree." The steward therefore gave judgment that he was to be freed from his allegiance to the Abbot of St Denis, and conceded to him "the right to remove to what wilderness I would. And this in the presence of the king and his servants was agreed and confirmed on either side." It had, perhaps, been a lucky day for Abelard when he lectured on Bede's *Exposition of the New Testament*.

XIX

Abelard was not the man to regard his monastic vows lightly, and he had no intention of abandoning them now that he had been released from his allegiance to St Denis. He took with him one friend and made his way to a hermitage on the Ardusson river in the desolate country near Troyes. There, in a cell or a cave, not far from the Troyes-Paris road and near to the little town of Nogent-sur-Seine, he took up his new abode.

But it is probable that he did not intend to cease from teaching, for though his hermitage lay in a wilderness it was designedly not too far from a road; and, likely enough, he let the place of his retirement be advertised among the Paris scholars. For no sooner had he arrived there than he was besieged by a vast and steady flow of scholars, who came demanding to be taught by him. Nor did he dismiss them.

Nothing could speak more eloquently both of the veneration in which learning was then held in Northern France and of Abelard's personal fame and his unceasing hold upon the imagination of youth than the extraordinary scenes which took place at his hermitage near Troyes in the three years 1122 to 1125. Importunate scholars flocked out of Paris, Rheims, and Orleans, and came to him demanding to be taught. But there were no buildings of any kind. Instead of living in the lodging-houses of the cities, they slept on the hard earth, until they could build little huts of clay and branches for themselves. Their beds were thatch and straw. Their food was the coarsest homemade bread, eked out by such herbs as they could gather, and the scanty provisions they could afford to buy at Nogent-sur-Seine. They ate it from tables rudely fashioned of heaped banks of turf. Such was their love for Abelard, and their avidity for his instruction, that, whatever discomforts they had at first to undergo themselves, their first concern was to see that he did not lack such material necessities as would set him free for study.

They built first a small oratory. But as their numbers increased it could hold only a few of them. They gradually, stage by stage, enlarged this oratory until at length it grew to a building of such size that it afterwards was used as a convent. But all this took time, and the work of building was not allowed to interrupt the general scheme of Abelard's teaching.

It was not until 1125 that the first rude oratory of clay gave way to the greater building of wood and stone. No sooner was it finished than Abelard, involved then in yet another bout of trouble, was forced to take the first opportunity of leaving it.

When he said that an evil fate was dogging his foot-steps it is hard not to believe him. For this new trouble was as absurd as the last, and as little sought by him. It can be passed over in a few words.

As the oratory was being built, the question of its ascription arose. Abelard resolved to dedicate it to the Holy Spirit, the Paraclete, Whose special function was that of comfort. It was a dedication thoroughly germane to his own circumstances, for the last three years had been of no small comfort to him. But his enemies were in no way appeased; and he, for his part, had certainly not abandoned his ambition to bring reason to the service of religion, as the general tenor of his teaching showed. Had anyone else chosen to dedicate a church to the Paraclete, even though the normal ascription was to the whole Trinity or to the Son alone, it would have escaped without notice. There were, after all, several priories ascribed to St Spirit. But Abelard had fathered it, and that by itself was quite enough to make people think that there must be a heresy concealed somewhere. The accusation was so ridiculous that he had little difficulty in show-ing that there could be no reasonable objection. No action followed the charge of unwarranted presump-tion, but his name was surrounded by even more suspicion than before.

But though the accusation was easily rebutted it left its scar on his mind. Living as he did upon his emotions, he began now to be the prey of nervous fantasies. It seemed that nothing he did could be right, as though it were possible for his enemies to twist the most innocent actions into occasions whereby their persecution might be renewed. In his troubles since he had left Heloise he could see only the malignancy of his enemies, and now, just when his fortunes had revived, came this hysterical charge, which, for all its hysteria, had again involved him in a fruitless combat. He was evidently surrounded by ill-will. In the mental panic which now overtook him, he magnified it into active persecution, and gave way to fanciful delusions.

Notably, his delusions took the form of imagining that his enemies had combined together to stir against him the two men who, above all others, were able to do him harm. "The one of them," he wrote, "boasted that he had reformed the life of the Canons Regular, the other that of the monks."

He did not mention their names, but it is obvious that he thought the first of these men was St Norbert. Norbert was one of the strangest figures of his time. He was a converted prebendary, who possessed all the convert's extremism, and whose uncritical enthusiasms led to bizarre, fantastic affectations of both beliefs and dress. He was the modern millenarist dressed in twelfth-century raiment, and was full of interpretations of the Apocalypse. This had brought upon him an accusation of heresy. But he won his case, and, though unable to reform his own chapter of canons, had retired to Prémontré, a solitude, and had there founded the famous order of Canons Regular in 1120. Tireless and self-confident, he had since become Archbishop of Magdeburg. His notoriety rested on his vital belief in the imminence of anti-Christ, for he rushed wildly about the country proclaiming his immediate arrival. He regarded all whose orthodoxy was not unimpeachable as the ambassadors of anti-Christ. There is an amusing letter of St Bernard's, written with all the gentle sarcasm of which, when he chose to use it, he was a past master.

> What you ask of me touching Norbert, whether he be going to Jerusalem, I cannot tell you. I saw him and spoke to him a few days ago, and from that heavenly flute—his voice—I heard many things, but on this point nothing at all. But when I spoke of anti-Christ and asked his opinion, he declared that he knew most certainly that he would be manifested during the very generation that now is. When I pressed him to give his reasons for his certitude, his answer was not of a kind to make me adopt his views as undoubted truth.[1]

There is no evidence beyond Abelard's bare statement that Norbert was ever aware of him. But Abelard was not the man of whom an Archbishop, who travelled widely and unceasingly in France, was likely to be unaware. And, most certainly, Norbert would violently have disapproved of everything he heard of him. His fear was not unreasonable, for Norbert, for all his absurdities, had power.

The second enemy of whom he spoke was the mighty

---

[1] Translated by Cotter Morison, *Saint Bernard*, p. 80.

and formidable St Bernard, Abbot of Clairvaux. Clairvaux was not far from Troyes, and the two institutions, representing the old and the new thought, competed in rivalry in the surrounding country. Thus St Bernard could not possibly have been unaware of Abelard. But of active enmity there was no visible sign yet. Bernard was to be the instrument which finally broke Abelard, but their titanic struggle had yet to come.

But to write that is to be wise after the event. It was not to be expected that Abelard should take so detached a view of the situation, nor, under the circumstances, that his view should exhibit a marked impartiality and balance. He was frankly terrified, and magnified every idle word, every irrelevant event into evidence of the subtle plots and machinations of his enemies. "God Himself is my witness," he wrote, "as often as I heard that any gathering of ecclesiastical persons had assembled; I imagined it to be purposing my condemnation."

It was an unhealthy but not an unnatural state of mind. He loved his school and he loved his scholars, but their solace did not compensate for his fears. Thus when there came an invitation, backed by the urgent requests of the Lord of the Manor and the Bishop of the Diocese, that he should return to his native Brittany as the abbot of the monastery of St Gildas de Ruys, he promptly consented. It seemed a Heaven-sent opportunity for him to escape from the neighbourhood of his fancied persecutors. He left his scholars, none the less, with regrets and a heavy heart. "Never (God wot) would I have acquiesced in this except that I might escape from those oppressions which, as I have said, I had incessantly to endure." Had he but known all that the next few years held in store, his heart would have been heavier still. For by his acceptance of his new office he entered what was to be by far the most calamitous period of his life.

XX

The abbacy of the monastery of St Gildas was considered to be a position of great honour, and in every way worthy of Abelard's reputation. Yet there could have been few twelfth-century functionaries less to be envied than the Abbot of St Gildas. The monastery was built on the southern coast of Brittany, about ten miles south of Vannes. Inland there lay a long stretch of hilly and desolate country. The peasants spoke a dialect so peculiar to themselves that Abelard, though himself a Breton, could never understand it. The feudal lord and his retainers were not untypical of the famous English barons during the reign of King Stephen. The monks of the abbey had sunk to a depth of profligacy which was hardly exceeded by the most notorious monasteries in the darkest days of the Church. In this it was hardly typical of the monastic institutions of its day, which, under the influence first of the Cluniac and then of the Cistercian revivals, had undergone a drastic purge. The trouble was possibly due to the fact that the abbey was, so to speak,

rather out of the world, being situated far away from
the centre of gravity of Church life in France. It is
significant that whereas at St Denis, and at his retreats
at both Maisoncelle and Troyes, Abelard had been
besieged by crowds of importunate scholars, there is
no record of such crowds ever besieging him at St
Gildas, in spite of the fact that immediately after his
years at the oratory of the Paraclete his fame as a
master stood higher than ever.

In Abelard's character there was an element of grim
determination which, as his conduct at St Denis had
shown, was specially aroused by the spectacle of living
hypocrisy. But whereas at St Denis he had been
merely one among many brethren, and, for all his
fame, held no recognised position, now he was the
abbot, and responsible for the spiritual and temporal
oversight of his monks. That element of robust determination had been lying dormant since the Council
of Soissons; but the bestowal upon him of a position
of authority, and a realisation of the bad ways into
which the abbey had lapsed, awakened it again, and
infused into his being a new vigour. He was determined to discharge his responsibility, however dangerous or difficult the task might be.

Certainly the task was both difficult and dangerous.
The monks had taken vows of chastity and poverty.
They all kept their own private purses; and they all
supported mistresses. Finding these expensive, they
stole and sold anything of value in the abbey on which
they could lay their hands. They pledged in the
abbey's name, and by the unauthorised perquisites

of such offices as they held, the jewels and the altar ornaments to Jewish moneylenders. They had mortgaged the abbey itself. The only property of the abbey left untouched by the monks was the land which belonged to it. This had escaped their depredations simply because the local nobleman, making the disorder of the abbey his excuse, had already seized all the estates and was impounding all the rents. Not content with this, he was pressing all kinds of exactions upon the monks.

Such was the situation with which Abelard was called to deal. Trying first to recall the monks from the evil of their ways, he did all he could by exhortation, expostulation, by prayer and by punishment. It was vain. Their ways continued to be extremely evil. He then tried the expedient of placing the worst offenders under discipline. That, too, was useless. Instead of being properly abashed, they merely plotted to murder him. "In the very sacrament of the altar they endeavoured to destroy me, putting poison in the chalice."

After the failure of this attempt, he had to travel to Nantes, and, as was the custom, he took two or three monks with him. Those whom he had put under discipline saw another chance. They bribed his servant to put poison in his food. But it happened that, before he touched the food, one of the monks with him, who knew nothing of the plot, helped himself and began to eat. He immediately fell ill with agonising and contorting pains, and swiftly died. The monks had taught Abelard to exercise all vigilance while in the abbey: they had hoped that once away he would relax his precaution.

Whether his former fears were fanciful or not, there was no doubt that he now moved in a grim reality of peril of death. As often happens, the danger braced him. There was no sign of quailing. He took the obvious precaution of sleeping close to, but outside the abbey walls, and of preparing his own food. Not even so was he safe, for when he went on any journey the monks hired robbers to attack him.

Threatening and expostulation having alike failed to effect any improvement, he now tried new methods. He appealed to their own interests. He pointed out to them how they were oppressed by the nobleman who had illegally impounded their rents, and appealed to them to forget their enmities in a concerted action against the common enemy of them all. He suggested that the best method of approach would be the removal of the excuse of their shameful ways of living, on which the tyrant had based his case. Thus he hoped to solve both his problems by one astute move.

But that, too, was vain. The monks hated him too much. Not even to save themselves from oppression would they stand by their accursed abbot. Nor would the people of the neighbourhood, who had suffered even more cruelly from this tyrant, join themselves with an abbot who was plainly not strong enough to protect them against his revenge.

Abelard was baffled, and the threats and attempts at murder continued unabated. For several years this state of affairs went on, until, at last, matters became

so serious that he determined to make use of the last
dread weapon, excommunication. He threatened the
worst offenders with the Church's ban. So great and
universal throughout Christendom was the dread of
it that even these hardened ruffians were for the time
brought to their senses. Under pain of excommunication he made them swear in the presence of witnesses
that they would leave the abbey and thenceforth trouble
him no more. Awestruck at such a threat, and their
abbot's manifest determination to put it into practice,
they departed.

But their awestruck mood passed as they found living
in the world less easy than they had supposed. With
its passing, they promptly violated the oaths they had
sworn, and returned to St Gildas again. Then, for the
first time, Abelard sought outside help. He appealed
to the Pope, who sent his Legate to hear the case.

The Legate summoned the monks, the tyrannical
count, and the bishop of the diocese. He forced the
recalcitrant monks to renew their promise that they
would go away, and trouble St Gildas no more. Yet
not even then did they remain quiet. They departed
once more, and the power of the lay authority, who had
been a party to the agreement, prevented them from
returning openly. But they stayed not far away, and
managed to stir up the brethren who were left. Between them they concocted a plan to cut Abelard's
throat. Timely news of it came to him. It was
revealed that the whole abbey was party to the plot.
At last, on hearing this, he fled away from St Gildas
and escaped.

There was nothing else left to do. He had tried every possible expedient, and all had failed. He had fought a good fight for nine years. He had lived in the midst of constant danger from 1125 to 1134. As though recognising the fact, the bishop made no difficulty in allowing him to retain the rank and title of abbot, and in releasing him from his charge.

It was then, just after he had fled from St Gildas, and when, in addition, he was racked with pain, having fallen from his horse and hurt his spine, the sense of failure lying heavy upon him, that he wrote *Historia Calamitatum*. Is it any wonder that gloom is the dominant note of it?

XXI

Abelard's nine years at St Gildas might well have cost him his sanity had their strain and gloom not been alleviated by certain distractions. After he had been there for a little over two years, however, circumstances threw him into a new bitter-sweet contact with Heloise, which, with its inevitable resurgence of the strongest emotions, rekindled the fires of his energy of spirit.

Since the day of her formal profession eight years before she had remained in the convent at Argenteuil. All that time she believed, as did Abelard, that their parting had been final in this world, and that she was doomed to spend the rest of her life at Argenteuil. And so, no doubt, it would have happened had not Suger, a great administrator who was destined to be the regent of the kingdom, succeeded to the abbacy of St Denis on the death of Adam, the abbot who had so tormented Abelard.

Suger had in his youth been a monk in the abbey, and the office he then held had given him access to its records. While exploring these documents he had noticed an old deed of King Clothaire III's, by which the Convent of Argenteuil and its lands had been assigned and granted to the Abbey of St Denis. For various reasons the deed of gift had not been put into operation at the time of its granting, and had since been forgotten. But it had never been cancelled, and, legally speaking, it was still perfectly valid. On being appointed abbot, Suger remembered his find, and determined at once to take action upon it.

He was *persona grata* with the king of France, Louis VI, and also with Pope Honorius II, and he had little difficulty in obtaining their powerful support for his claims. Moreover, it could not be denied that they were perfectly legal. It only remained to reinforce the legal right by a moral sanction. This Suger did by accusing the convent of some minor disorders which he was able to prove to the satisfaction of the visiting bishop and the legate whom the Pope sent to inquire into the case. Thus armed, he had no difficulty in persuading the Pope to ratify his claim on Argenteuil, which was duly done by a Papal Bull dated 1127. The Bull does not seem to have made any provision for the nuns.

They were promptly dispossessed and driven away, while Suger took possession. Some, including the abbess, entered the convent of Notre Dame des Bois. Others renounced their vows to live monastically and re-entered the world. Those who were still left, looking now to Heloise as their natural leader, wandered round France, begging their way, and seeking some convent to take them in.

News of all this came eventually to Abelard's ears, but he is tantalisingly silent about how it came. Mr George Moore postulates a chance meeting between the lovers in a tavern where Abelard was lodging on a journey and Heloise had come to beg for food. Seizing his chance, he builds upon the supposition one of the most haunting and memorable scenes in English fiction. But it is supposition. Abelard, at times so prolix in his writing, maintains an infuriating silence about an event on which, almost above all others, we should like to satisfy our curiosity. But while the imagination must be left to picture the meeting, the facts which followed from it are plain enough.

When he had gone to St Gildas the oratory of the Paraclete had been abandoned. The scholars went their ways, leaving it empty and still. But, empty or not, it was his; and at that moment the fact of its existence seemed providential. He gave it to Heloise and the nuns with her, surrendering to her "all things pertaining thereto." He asked her to become the abbess, and in 1129 the Bishop of Troyes approved the gift and arrangement.

It seemed wise, however, to have the gift sanctioned by an even higher authority; and in 1131 the chance came.

Pope Honorius was dead, and with the election of the new Pope Innocent II a schism had arisen. Innocent had been forced to flee to France, owing to the strength of the anti-Pope's territorial connections in Italy. There he had been received and acclaimed by St Bernard, by Peter of Cluny, and by the king himself. Escorted by them, he began a triumphal tour through the country. He came to Chartres, receiving there Bishop Geoffrey and Henry I of England; and from there set out for Liége, where he was to meet the Emperor. On the way he stayed for two days at the abbey at Morigny. His purpose there was to consecrate a church; and gathered to meet him was a notable company—cardinals, bishops, and abbots. Among them was Peter Abelard. His moment came, and he petitioned the Pope to ratify the gift of the Bishop of Troyes. The Pope promised, and in due course the document of ratification came, confirming for ever the gift of the oratory of the Paraclete to the Abbess Heloise and a company of twenty-nine nuns. It was at Morigny that Abelard first met face to face the man who was to dominate the rest of his life, Bernard of Clairvaux. They were easily the two greatest figures of the Church in France. It would almost seem as though, sensing the conflict that had yet to come, they stood each gazing appraisingly at the other, estimating his strength.

Abelard stood in a special relationhip to what now was the Abbey of the Paraclete. He had given the abbey and he was the husband of the abbess. He was thus doubly responsible; and it fell to him, burdened as he already was by the cares of St Gildas, to make provision for their needs. Besides this, Heloise, always eager to devise chains to bind him to her, requested that he should assume as well a spiritual oversight. She was still but twenty-nine, and she showed a talent for practical administration worthy of her reputation for learning. "The bishops loved her as a daughter, the abbots as a sister, the laity as a mother. All alike marvelled at her piety, her prudence, and, in all things, the incomparable meekness of her patience."

But at first poverty was the lot of the new congregation, and the country folk began to murmur that Abelard might have helped them more than he did. In this respect there was little he could do which Heloise could not do better, and he was fighting a tremendous battle with himself, trying to make himself regard her as his sister in Christ rather than his wife. But his knowledge of their poverty, coupled with the extreme wretchedness of his situation at St Gildas, constrained him to make frequent journeys to his old oratory. Very soon the ill-conditioned oafs at St Gildas began to seize the opportunity to spread abroad scandalous suggestions. One would have thought that his physical condition, which almost everyone knew, would have been sufficient to save him from leering innuendos of the sort. But it was not so; and though he felt the suggestions keenly he did not allow them to affect the frequency of his visits.

But he showed that he was deeply wounded by the passion with which he defended himself. And, indeed, he probably felt that his position was a false one, not in so much that he, Abelard, was visiting his wife, Heloise, but because the Church frowned upon any abbot having many direct dealings with a congregation of women. His defence against this "insult of detraction" was made at great length and with a passionate vehemence. In the course of it he made the interesting suggestion, amply buttressed by instances drawn from the early days of the Church, that the Church of his day was departing from the precedents both of the Fathers and the Apostles in thus decrying the ministrations of men to women. It was a thrust characteristic of his earlier days, and a sign that the salt of a righteous conflict with his monks and the precious contact with Heloise had begun to heal his wounds. Abelard was becoming himself again. He continued to balance the miseries of St Gildas by his work of succouring the newly founded abbey of the Paraclete.

XXII

When Abelard at last fled from the Abbey of St Gildas he was an ageing man of fifty-eight. He felt the burden of his years all the more by reason of the physical pain which followed from his accident. He was certainly not free from danger, for the monks he had expelled from the abbey were breathing threatenings and slaughter, and he had had sufficient experience of them to know that they would not scruple to put their threats into practice if they had the chance. Under these circumstances he deemed it wise to remain in hiding. Where his hiding-place was situated is not known; but very probably it was within easy reach of the Abbey of the Paraclete. In the country around the city of Troyes there were a multitude of places where a man might lie concealed.

He was urged to this retirement by another consideration, the need of putting his intellectual house in order. The last ten years had immersed him in the more immediate affairs of the administrator. But he had never forgotten his ambition to show religion's vital need of reason and himself to fill the gap. During the year, 1135, which he spent as it were in retreat, he wrote furiously. Every kind of composition sped under his pen, books on theology, poems, hymns, treatises on the monastic life, and, among them, the *Historia Calamitatum* and the letters to Heloise by which the world chiefly knows him.

At this point it will be convenient to pause, as his life paused, to consider this large and varied mass of his literary activity.

XXIII

The *Historia Calamitatum* was written in the form of a letter to a friend, and it begins:

> Often examples serve better than words to excite or to mitigate human passions. Wherefore, after certain comfort offered thee in speech in thy presence, I have decided in absence to write by way of comfort the

experience of my own calamities, that in comparison of
mine thou mayest see thy trials to be none at all, or but
slight matters, and may be better able to endure them.

Then follows the whole story of his life up to the time
of his writing. This short introduction sets the
atmosphere of the whole, for it is charged with egoism
and self-pity. The document which follows it is one
of almost unalleviated gloom. While reading it one's
irritation with the writer grows and grows until one
is driven to explain it in the most charitable way one
can by declaring it to be the product of a diseased
mind. Having regard to the facts of his life during the
fifteen years previous to his writing of it, and the
constant emotional strain under which he had been
living, to say that the *Historia Calamitatum* betokens
a temporarily diseased mind is probably not only
charitable but also true. The peering introspection
it betokens was morbid, and suffered from all the
limitations of morbidity. For page after page, he
accused himself, he pitied himself, and, certainly, he
distorted himself. Calamity is heaped upon calamity,
woe upon woe, complaint upon complaint, until the
tale seems forced and strained, and the reader has to
be perpetually reminding himself of the circumstances
in which the document was written. Taken at its
face value, the *Historia Calamitatum* reveals a querulous,
quarrelsome, boastful, and whining old man.

The document is one which no biographer of
Abelard will ever be able to escape, because it is an
invaluable record of the objective facts. But no
biographer can be comfortable with it, because, when

used as evidence for anything more than the bare facts, it becomes a snare and a delusion. Many writers have been led astray by relying blindly upon Abelard's own words. Cotter Morison, as has already been shown, was content to accept Abelard's own account of his courting of Heloise, and to draw from it damaging conclusions which, when challenged by Lane Poole, he afterwards had to repudiate. Yet Abelard's account did, when uncritically read, involve those very strictures. Scott-Moncrieff uses its evidence to conclude that

> the young cocksure who confuted William of Champeau and laughed in the venerable beard of Anselm has dwindled into a querulous craven, constantly in terror of persecution, poison, and the rest, magnifying his dangers with a buoyant indifference to his correspondent's natural anxiety.[1]

Yet the facts of history are in themselves sufficient to dispel such a ludicrously limited view. Querulous cravens do not make history, do not mould the habits of thought of future generations, do not draw young scholars in thousands to them, do not need the terrific authority of a St Bernard to quell them, and do not win the undying love of women like Heloise. Abelard did all of these things.

The *Historia Calamitatum* is, and is likely to remain as puzzling on psychological as it is on critical grounds. The wisest and probably the final judgment is that of Lane Poole. He is writing about Abelard's account of his love for Heloise, but what he says is applicable

---

[1] *The Letters of Abelard and Heloise*, p. 11. (Guy Chapman.)

to the whole psychological problem raised by the *Historia Calamitatum* :

> Abailard himself, our sole informant of the particulars of his love for Heloissa (I adopt his spelling of their names), was a man whose self-reliance . . . required that every act of his should seem to be a skilfully devised link in a consistent chain of policy; he almost writes as if to persuade us that from the outset he deliberately planned his mistress's ruin. To those who read his words with a deeper perception of character, and much more to those who go on to the long correspondence and the lifelong interdependence of Abailard and Heloissa, such an explanation will appear not merely inadequate but incredible. Abailard's account, written moreover under the oppression of enduring remorse, is too highly coloured by these mixed feelings to be taken as it stands : his interpretation of his error, or his guilt, is misleading.[1]

That is finely and justly said. It should be pondered by those who are over-ready to rush in with their condemnations. The ground on which they are treading is certainly not holy, but it is none the less wise to tread delicately.

The document, so Abelard said, was a letter to a friend. He did not name the friend; and about this document and the letters to which it forms the background there hang considerable critical difficulties, which it will be more convenient to consider later. Whatever the genesis of the document, however, it fell into Heloise's hands. Her answer to it is one of the most famous letters in the world. This letter of hers, and the one that followed his answer to it, defy analysis. On them depend the fame of their story. Without

---

[1] *Illustrations of the History of Mediæval Thought and Learning*, pp. 124, 125. (S.P.C.K.)

the letters it would be possible to regard it as a sordid affair of treachery, intrigue, unbridled lust, and almost as a repellent barbaric romance. But the letters lift it into another plane. They save it from being turned into a moralist's tale, and being used as an example of the fate awaiting those who give rein too freely to their lusts. More than anything else, it is the two first letters of Heloise rather than of Abelard that lift their story into regions not far from sublime. They are beyond praise, and they defy description. They quiver with beauty which rends the reader. It is better to quote. Here is the passage which ends the first letter:

> Not with me was my heart but with thee. But now, more than ever, if it be not with thee, it is nowhere. For without thee it cannot anywhere exist. But so act that it may be well with thee, I beseech thee. And well with thee will it be if it find thee propitious, if thou give love for love, little for much, words for deeds. Would that thy love, beloved, had less trust in me, that it might be more anxious. But the more confident I have made thee in the past, the more neglectful now I find thee. Remember, I beseech thee, what I have done and pay heed to what thou owest me. While with thee I enjoyed carnal pleasures, many were uncertain whether I did so from love or from desire. But now the end shows in what spirit I began. I have forbidden myself all pleasures that I might obey thy will. I have reserved nothing for myself, save this, to be now entirely thine. Consider therefore how great is thine injustice, if to me who deserve more thou payest less, nay nothing at all, especially when it is a small thing that is demanded of thee, and right easy to perform.
>
> And so in His Name to whom thou hast offered thyself, before God I beseech thee that in whatsoever way thou

canst thou restore to me thy presence, to wit by writing me some word of comfort. To this end alone that, thus refreshed, I may give myself with more alacrity to the service of God. When in time past thou soughtest me out for temporal pleasures, thou visitedst me with endless letters, and with frequent songs didst set thy *Heloise* on the lips of all men. With me every public place, each house resounded. How more rightly shouldst thou excite me now towards God, whom thou excitedst then to desire. Consider, I beseech thee, what thou owest me, pay heed to what I demand; and my long letter with a brief ending I conclude. Farewell, my all.

Abelard's reply was evasive. She had asked him before all else to write to her, and he at once complied with the request. But his tone was rigorously austere. He dared not write in the vein of the ending of her letter. There were certain memories which must remain buried. He was an abbot and she an abbess. They had been lovers; but they were now brother and sister in Christ. Irretrievably committed, he dared not encourage himself to think of a closer relationship. So, writing as an abbot to an abbess, he is full of pious exhortations. Only once is the mask lifted. "If the Lord should deliver me into the hands of mine enemies, so that they prevail over me and slay me . . . wheresoever, I beseech you, my body may lie, have it brought to your cemetery."

But even that slight lifting of the mask was too much. For Heloise, putting aside the rest of the letter, picked upon that one slight revelation of the deep passions surging underneath, and upon it based her second letter. "O, dearest, with what mind didst thou think that, with what lips couldst thou endure to say it.   Never may God so forget His handmaids as to keep them to survive thee."   She dwelt upon that pain for many pages, and then turned to the remarkable confession of her inherent unfitness for her office, from which quotation has already been made.   His trust in her was misplaced, she protested.

> Always, I beseech thee, be fearful for me rather than place thy trust in me, that I may ever be helped by thy solicitude.   But now especially must thou fear, when no remedy is left in thee for my incontinence.   I wish not that, exhorting me to virtue, and provoking me to fight, thou say: "Strength is made perfect in weakness"; and: "Yet is he not crowned, unless he strive lawfully."   I seek not a crown of victory.   It is enough for me to avoid danger.   It is safer to avoid danger than to engage in battle.

The motive for Abelard's earlier guarded reserve had been his desire to serve their common happiness, which, he was convinced, lay in an ungrudging acceptance of their present situation.   But this second letter from Heloise broke all the barriers he had erected. He sat down to answer it, and for many pages forced himself to bury his feelings and to write formally as before.   He warned her of the dangers that encompassed the path of those who brooded longingly over joys that had once been, but which could not be again. He set before her the guilt that their love had involved; and as he did so his reserve suddenly broke down. For the first time he wrote as he felt, dropping the disguise, and revealing a heart which ached no less than her own, and a purpose even more steadfast.

> Take heed, therefore, take heed, beloved, with what drawnets of His mercy, from the depths of this so

perilous sea the Lord fished us up, and from the gullet of what a Charybdis. He has saved our ship-wrecked, albeit unwilling souls. . . . Think, and think again, in what dangers we were placed, and from what dangers the Lord plucked us out: and repeat always with the utmost thanksgiving what things the Lord has done for our soul. . . . Perpend the supreme designs of divine piety towards us, and how mercifully the Lord has turned His Judgment into regeneration, and how prudently He has made use of the evil also, and piously deposed impiety. . . . Compare the danger and the manner of deliverance. Compare the sickness and the medicine. Examine the cause—our deserts—and marvel at the effect, His mercy.

Compared with Heloise's unchecked passion, this has a graver beauty. But it is beauty none the less. The letter continues for many pages, until at last it rises to an exaltation of religious devotion when Abelard, throwing all restraint to the winds, comes to a majestic climax in prayer:

God, Who from the first beginning of the human creation, with woman formed from the rib of man didst sanctify the great sacrament of the nuptial bond, and Who hast raised marriage to the greatest honour . . . despise not the prayer of thine handmaid, which for mine own excesses and for those of my beloved in the sight of thy Majesty I pour forth in supplication. Pardon, O most bountiful, nay bounty itself: pardon our so great offences, and may the ineffable immensity of Thy Mercy make trial of the multitude of our faults. . .

Thou hast joined us together, O Lord, and Thou hast put us asunder when it pleased Thee and in the manner that pleased Thee. Now, O Lord, what thou hast mercifully begun most mercifully finish. And these who thou hast divided one from another once upon earth join perenni-ally to Thyself in Heaven. Our hope, our portion, our expectation, our comfort, Lord Who art Blessed, world without end. AMEN.

Farewell in Christ, Bride of Christ, in Christ farewell, and in Christ dwell. AMEN.

This letter set an end to the passionate outpourings of Heloise, and she accepted the inevitable. But she did not cease from writing. He would not be the lover, but he was still the protector of her convent, and she wrote asking for instructions, for a rule of life for the nuns, for a history of their order, for a set of hymns for them to sing. She was not even then satisfied, for she sent forty-two knotty points of theology for him to solve; and we find him writing for her and her nuns a series of sermons, and the *Hexameron*, an examination from a theological standpoint of the *Genesis* account of creation. These were all safe requests, and with all of them Abelard gladly and swiftly complied. The rest of their correspondence deals wholly with matters such as these. Abelard, busy though he was with other work, spared no pains to gratify her lightest request. In all ways save one, he showed himself passionately anxious to please her.

XXIV

"The love letters of Heloise were not written by a mediæval woman but were the vain imaginings of a very vain man." [1]

This sentence occurs in the course of review of

---

[1] *Speculum*, vol. ii, p. 227.

The Legacy of the Middle Ages, which was published in Volume II of the American Journal *Speculum*. The writer, an American professor, does not disclose the grounds on which he bases this remarkable judgment, but throws it out by the way, and passes immediately to something else. It is a good example of the *Reductio ad Absurdum* of criticism. Had he said that possibly the letter contained forged elements, had he even said that the whole of the letters were untrustworthy evidence for history, he would have made a statement that was at least arguable. But to say that Abelard deliberately invented the entire correspondence with the intention of surrounding his name with a romantic glamour that was never his in reality is about as sensible as to suggest that Heloise never existed. To read the letters in such a way is to make nonsense of them at every point. To charge Abelard with such a forgery is to make his whole life and character unintelligible. The truth about the letters is certainly obscure, but to suggest that Abelard invented them all is to charge him with what it is incredible that he had the capacity to do even if he had the will. Such statements darken counsel.

None the less, there are difficulties, for these letters have had a curious history. About a hundred years after they were written they were translated from their original Latin by Jean de Meung, a dissolute young blackguard, who was also a poet of genius. Since that time they have passed through countless editions. The oldest now existing is a Latin edition, printed in Paris in 1616, a copy of which is in the British

Museum. That is the text used by Scott-Moncrieff for his authoritative and definitive translation of 1925, from which all the extracts used in this book are taken. His translation, therefore, is as near to the original as we are ever likely to get.

But there have been other English translations, notably the very inaccurate one of 1722, which contains some astonishing blunders. It was this edition which gave the name Philintus to Abelard's correspondent of the first letter, the *Historia Calamitatum*, and though that does not matter very much in practice, there are pages and pages of interpolations, including a totally imaginary account of how the lovers were betrayed to Fulbert by Heloise's maid, who had herself fallen in love with Abelard, and had been repulsed by him. It also omits more than half of what the lovers wrote. From these absurdities Scott-Moncrieff has rescued English readers. Though it is to be feared that most people's knowledge of the letters is gained from this 1722 edition, for that is the edition used for the version of the letters in the *Temple Classics*.

Now the *Historia Calamitatum* is written in the form of a letter to an unnamed friend. It came into Heloise's hand, and formed the excuse for the rest of the correspondence. It is assumed by Scott-Moncrieff that the unnamed friend was Heloise. From that assumption two things follow, first, that that part of her reply where she writes with horror-stricken grief of his fell news is a forgery, since she must have known all about it already, having many times met Abelard after her expulsion from Argenteuil; second, and alternatively, that the whole of the *Historia Calami-tatum* is a forgery, committed presumably by Jean de Meung, and designed to create a background for the genuine letters which follow it.

Of these alternatives, the first is possible, but the second raises psychological difficulties so grave that it may be dismissed. Mr George Moore, who writes an introductory letter to Scott-Moncrieff's translation, is inclined to think that the first paragraph of Heloise's first letter is a forgery, but that the rest is genuine. And, apart from one or two isolated passages, he is convinced of the genuineness of the *Historia Calami-tatum*. He writes:

> Her first letter to him begins: "Your letter addressed to a friend for his comfort was lately brought to me by chance." By chance! She must have known of his mutilation when they rode to Troyes.[1]

But though horror and grief are certainly present in her letter, there is little real suggestion of amazement or of ignorance of his calamities. There is nothing inconsistent with a previous knowledge of them.

If therefore it is assumed that Abelard really was writing to a friend, as he said, and not to Heloise, the assumption would seem to rid us of the necessity of regarding a part of her letter as a forgery. It does not seem an unreasonable assumption, and it avoids doing violence to the psychological probabilities. It may not be easy to explain after an interval of six hundred years how the letter came into her hands, but a thousand accidents can be imagined which would

[1] *Op. cit.*, p. 15.

account for it. This suggestion does not, of course, clear away the difficulties over certain passages in the letter. They can hardly be satisfactorily explained without more evidence than exists.

Another possible suggestion is that the *Historia Calamitatum*, though written in the form of a letter, was really a literary composition cast in that form, as to-day "Open Letters" are sometimes ostensibly addressed to politicians, but are really newspaper articles. Such a supposition implies no insincerity in the writer. In that case the *Historia Calamitatum* becomes an attempt at a short autobiography, and possibly written under the impulse of the need to find an outlet for the psychological disturbances welling under the surface of Abelard's mind, which his troubles had produced.

However that may be, the document did have the effect of probing a sore and letting out some of the festering matter. By thoroughly indulging his emotions in an unrestrained expression of them, Abelard to some extent cured himself of his morbidity. For in the other writings which he put forth whilst still in his retreat he showed himself once more strong and sane; and he fitted himself the better for the last and greatest of his conflicts.

XXV

During the year Abelard spent in his hidden retreat after his flight from St Gildas, we may picture him, then, as using his pen to compose into a harmony his different indwelling emotions, which, by the urgency of their clamour, were tending towards his mental and spiritual impoverishment.

Like many other men of abnormal sensitiveness, he was an artist at bottom; and, as another means of giving expression to the turmoil and urgency in his mind, he turned again to poetry. Years before, in the days of his wild, tumultuous joy, when the fame of the schools seemed well lost for the love of Heloise, he had sought to express in poetry the beauty he found in living. But the lyrics of that time and mood have perished. Probably he destroyed them himself, for to that memory, as Miss Helen Waddell says, "he was merciless, and one may be sure that no fragment of the love songs would be found among his papers." If any memory survives, it is, as she asserts, "here and there in the anonymous song books of the century" where "a lyric may have caught something of the shattering ecstasy of their fire."

> "Take thou this rose, O rose,
> Since love's own flower it is,
> And by that rose
> Thy lover captive is." [1]

It is the shadow of a lost glory—no more.

Desolation, loneliness, and perplexity are moods no less urgent, and, as the splendid tale of elegies shows, no less apt for poetic expression. Abelard, turning again to his Muse, now composed a series of six laments. It is in keeping with his changed view of life that they should all be inspired by biblical heroes.

[1] Helen Waddell, *The Wandering Scholars*, p. 197. (Constable.)

They were laments for Dinah, Jacob's daughter; for Jephthah's daughter, "dead in her virginity," pitiful victim of an insane oath; for David, weeping and beating his breast in his agony of grief for the death of Jonathan, his friend; for Israel, mourning Samson; for David, weeping for Abner. In each of them the story is interwoven with reflections upon his own unhappy state. They are perfect expressions of a state of mind, faultless in taste, poignant in beauty. Miss Waddell has made a superb translation of one of the plaints, that of David for Jonathan.

> Low in thy grave with thee
> Happy to lie,
> Since there's no greater thing left Love to do :
> And to live after thee
> Is but to die ;
> For with but half a soul what can Life do ?
>
> To share thy victory,
> Or else thy grave,
> Either to rescue thee, or with thee lie :
> Ending that life for thee,
> That thou didst save
> So death that sundereth might bring more nigh.
>
> Peace, O my stricken lute !
> Thy strings are sleeping.
> Would that my heart could still
> Its bitter weeping ! [1]

David for Jonathan? Or Abelard, unable for all his effort, to still his passion for Heloise?

Among the requests which Heloise wrote to him was one that he should compose a collection of hymns and sequences to be sung by the nuns in the Paraclete.

[1] Helen Waddell, *Mediæval Latin Lyrics*, p. 169. (Constable.)

At first resisting on the ground that it was impiety
to seek to add to or to improve the time-honoured
rhythms of the Fathers, he eventually yielded and set
himself to the task. To judge by the standard of
very many of the hymns which are sung Sunday by
Sunday in our churches, there is no form of poetic
expression which, seeming more easy, is in fact more
difficult. The expression of religious devotion so
easily becomes sentimental and weak, and the poetry
of divine mystery can so swiftly sink into vagueness
or atavism. Yet Abelard undertook to compose a
whole series, a hymn-book of his own, and he accomplished it with real success.

He would not have been Abelard had not the form
of some of the verses been experimental, and not all
of the experiments were happy. The metre of some
of the hymns set for Matins moves heavily.

> Deus qui tuos erudis
> Testamentorum paginis
> Ex eorum intelligentiæ
> Cantus nostros condis dulcedine.

The hymns for the other canonical hours, Lauds, Prime,
Terce, Sext, Compline, and Vespers are mostly written
in twelve-syllable rhymed couplets, as in the lovely

> O quanta qualia, sunt illa sabbata
> Quæ semper celebrat superna curia,

so familiar to every Anglican worshipper in J. M.
Neale's translation:

> O what their joy and their glory must be,
> Those endless Sabbaths the blessed ones see !
> Crowns for the valiant ; to weary ones rest ;
> God shall be all, and in all ever blest ;

and ending

> There dawns no Sabbath, no Sabbath is o'er,
> Those Sabbath keepers have one and no more ;
> One and unending is that triumph song
> Which to the angels and us shall belong.
>
> Low before Him with our praises we fall,
> Of whom, and in whom, and through whom are all ;
> Of whom, the Father ; and through whom, the Son ;
> In whom the Spirit, with these ever one.

But his most lovely verses are those which he often took almost word for word from the Bible. On Sundays at Lauds the nuns of the Paraclete sang this echo of the first Easter Morning.

> Transacto flebili de morte vespere,
> Cum vita redditur mane lætitiæ,
> Resurgit Dominus, apparent angeli
> Custodes fugiunt splendore territi.

Or, most exquisite of all, "In Rama was there a voice heard, lamentation, and weeping, and great mourning, Rachel weeping for her children, and would not be comforted because they are not." He scarcely altered a word.

> Est in Rama
> Vox audite
> Rachel flentis
> Super natos
> Interfectos
> Eiulantis
>
> Lacerata
> Iacent membra
> Parvulorum
> Et tam lacte
> Quam cruore
> Rigant humum.

XXVI

Abelard's chief preoccupation, however, during his later years at St Gildas and the year which followed them, was not the writing of his letters and instructions for Heloise, nor yet the expression of his spirit in poetry. It was the perfecting of his system of theology. He had already written the *Sic et Non*, and the *Introduction to Theology*, which had been condemned and burned by the Council of Soissons. To those works he now added three more, all of them of the first importance, a book on Ethics, called *Know Thyself*, a treatise, *Christian Theology*, and a commentary upon St Paul's *Epistle to the Romans*. In these five works is contained the body of his thought about religion, and it was on the doctrine contained in them that St Bernard seized, when he procured his final condemnation by the Council of Sens.

In the first half of the twelfth century there were, broadly speaking, two main schools of theological opinion and method. The first of them was mystical rather than intellectual, and its doctrinal emphasis was severely dogmatic and practical, in the sense that the world gives to those two words. Any matter upon which either authority or tradition had pronounced was not merely beyond question, but also beyond the necessity or even the desirability of explanation. Their methods, when administered by such men as St Bernard, were magnificently fruitful

of "souls saved unto salvation," but they had all the
drawbacks of innate and instinctive conservatism.
Thus, any approach to or flirting with the intoxicating
exercise of human reason was gravely suspect, even if
it was not heretical. The spiritual home of the school
was Citeaux; and its leading exponents were St
Bernard, Hildebert, Bishop of Mans, and William of
St Thierry. Bernard spoke for the theological trend
of the entire school of thought in his famous aphorism,
"Faith is not an opinion but a certitude."

The other leading school of theological thought was
as innately liberal as the first was conservative. It was
connected in its early stages with the name of William
of Champeau. He was so ardent a Realist that the
school was not particularly suspect so long as he
directed its fortunes. But even under him the
method of study was preponderantly dialectical, and
from dialectics to the exaltation of reason was but
a short and, in the end, an inevitable step. When
William had become a bishop, and was on intimate
terms with Bernard of Clairvaux, he regretted the
theological fashion he had encouraged at Paris, and
prophesied evil of it. As Abelard had stepped into
his shoes, his forebodings showed no great foresight,
for it must have been clear that the method of study
he had adopted with his pupils would, if its logical
implications were ruthlessly followed by a man of
genius, lead to just such a devastating application of
dialectic to religion as the *Sic et Non* had proved to be.
The members of this school of thought, of whom
Abelard, and, after him, his great pupil, Peter Lombard,

were the leaders, were called the Theorists. It is a
title of irritated contempt with history and human
nature written all over it. They devoted themselves
to speculative research on doubtful points of theology,
and to argumentative controversy over the more difficult questions of dogmatic faith.

Of these two schools, the Theorists held the key
to the future of theological thought, for their method
of approach was to be that of the prodigious intellect
of St Thomas Aquinas. But in Abelard's time the
mystics held the reins of power firmly in their hands,
and their leader St Bernard was in effect the un-
crowned king of Europe.

The Theorists had all been brought up in the
ceaseless study of the great philosophers. While
their learning was in no way confined to the writings
of Aristotle and Plato and their followers—Abelard,
for instance, quoted more readily from the Fathers—
they had made them so completely a part of their being
that they could not conceive that philosophy should
have nothing to say to the Catholic Faith. According
to their views, if it could be shown that the specula-
tions of Plato, arrived at by the light of pure reason,
had foreshadowed the doctrine of the Holy Trinity,
then the truth of that doctrine had been powerfully
reinforced. Any interpretation of it that pagan
philosophy could furnish as it were in advance was
as likely to be right as the interpretation of the most
inspired of the Fathers. Between the inspiration of
Plato and that of Jerome or Augustine was no difference in kind, and the more ardent spirits of the

Theorists would have denied even a difference in degree.

Such ideas held seeds of danger. For the Church had always been a little doubtful of the philosopher's aid, though it had never officially condemned it, and the more violently orthodox spirits of the twelfth century distrusted it very strongly. They were merely heirs of an undercurrent of suspicion which was hundreds of years old. St Paul had spoken bitterly of philosophers in his letters to the Romans and the Colossians. "Knowing God, they glorified him not as God, neither gave thanks; but became vain in their reasonings, and their senseless heart was darkened" (Rom. i. 21). " Take heed lest there shall be anyone that maketh spoil of you through his philosophy and vain deceit, after the tradition of men, after the rudiments of the world" (Col. ii. 8). If that does not amount to a formal condemnation of all philosophy, it at least betokens a suspicion of it. Moreover, while such Fathers of the Church as Justin, Clement, and the always perturbing Origen had welcomed the help that philosophy could give to religion, others had asserted firmly that philosophy could only be a hindrance and a snare. Gregory of Nazianzen had rued the day when "the perverted art of Aristotle had slipped into the Church." Tertullian had inveighed against the Athenian wisdom, and had denounced a stoic, platonic, or dialectical interpretation of the Faith. "The philosophers are the patriarchs of heresy. Miserable Aristotle!" Other Fathers agreed. Was not Arius a dialectician? Had not

Themistius, the great peripatetic, fathered the Gnostic errors?

Philosophy tended to Reason: Reason tended to Heresy: therefore Philosophy tended to Heresy. If the full stream of the Church's tradition did not give authority to the truth of the syllogism, at least a part of the authoritative tradition supported it. Bernard, and those who shared with him the effective authority of the Church of the twelfth century, took their stand uncompromisingly with Tertullian. To them, philosophy as applied to the elucidation of the essential mysteries of Christianity was contrary to the established order, if it was not itself heretical. They would cheerfully have said what Savonarola said three centuries later, "Any old woman knows more of saving grace than Plato."

Philosophy, called variously "profane science" and "secular learning," is not merely applicable to religion; religion has vital need of its services. Every doctrine of Christianity must be tested by reason. In those two sentences is contained the heart of Abelard's approach to theology. "I love profane science for its grace and beauty," he said, "and of this slave—a captured stranger—I wish to make an Israelite." And not philosophy only, but literature, and the whole range of the liberal education, he brought into his study, and held himself justified in so doing. Another dictum of his makes it clear. "The Synod of Pope Eugenius in the time of Louis [A.D. 826, Synod of Rome] positively ordered the study and teaching of literature and the liberal arts, and if St Jerome was punished by the Lord for having read the works of Cicero, it was because he read them simply for his own pleasure."

The heights to which Abelard exalted theology's necessity of reason are clearly shown in a famous passage.

How far are they worthy of attention who assert that faith is not to be built up or defended by reasoning?

Now very many persons seek to console themselves for their ignorance, when they are endeavouring to inculcate those points of faith which they are not even able to discuss in intelligible terms, by recommending that exceeding zealous faith which believes before it comprehends what is said, before it can perceive what the matter in hand really is, and whether it should be acknowledged as worthy of acquiescence, or discussed before it is received.

But they assert this chiefly in topics connected with the nature of the Deity, and the divisibility of the Holy Trinity, which they declare can never be understood in this life; but they say that the very understanding of this is eternal life, according to that word of truth which says: "And this is life eternal, that they should know thee the only true God, and Jesus Christ, whom thou hast sent" (John xvii. 3). And again, "I will manifest myself unto him" (John xiv. 21). But, surely, to understand a belief is one thing; to know or make manifest another.

Faith, therefore, is defined as the evidence of things not seen; experience as the knowledge of existing things by the very presence of the things themselves. Between these two St Gregory distinguishes in his Sixth Homily on the Gospels, in Book II, when he says: "It is manifest, because faith is the evidence of such things as cannot be seen, for those things which are seen are known, not believed."

Also the word "intellect" is properly applied as concerning those things which are invisible; for there is a distinction between the natures of things intellectual and things visible. Whoever, therefore, supposes that topics connected with the Trinity cannot be understood even in this life is lapsing into that false doctrine of Montanus, the heretic, which Jerome condemns in the preface to his Commentaries upon Isaiah where he says: "Nor, in truth, as Montanus dreams, did the prophets speak in an ecstasy," as men who did not understand what they were uttering, and as those who, when they had learned from others, were ignorant of what they themselves were saying.

It was entirely characteristic, though hardly tactful of Abelard to defend his position by indulging in a thrust at the position of the members of the opposite camp.

In the point of view there outlined is no taint of heresy, and though to say that the mystery of the Holy Trinity is not ideally beyond the power of human understanding must have sounded bold and presumptuous in the ears of the Cistercians at Clairvaux, it was not more than that. But it was what his position might involve that was frightening to churchmen who, if they did not share Norbert's extravagant beliefs, saw the recent schism in the Papacy, and the dark sea of heresy that was Provence, and felt that only the unquestioning unity of the faithful believers could save the Christian civilisation from disruption. Abelard seemed to them to be starting from exactly the same position, the exaltation of human reason, whence the Albigensians had set out. If he had remained content with elaborating finely drawn distinctions between Faith, Experience, and Intellect, he might have escaped the final *débâcle*. But when, in two famous aphorisms, he summed up the whole of his teaching on the relation of reason to religion, and phrased them so succinctly that they could hardly be forgotten by anyone who had once heard them, he was inviting trouble. The two aphorisms would sound startling even in a twentieth-century book of theology. With what a shock must they have struck on twelfth-century ears. They were, "By doubting we are led to inquire: by inquiry we perceive the truth," and, more startling still, "A doctrine is not to be believed because God has said it, but because we are convinced by reason that it is so." It does not require any great power of imagination to understand the effect of such remarks as these on the eager minds of students, who had come to believe in the plenary inspiration of his lightest word. They would see to it that his boldness received a wide publicity.

But while the more indiscreet among his followers interpreted his words as meaning that in his scheme of things human reason reigned alone, unassisted by the supernatural power of the divine revelation, he himself failed logically to pursue the meaning of his words to that extreme. He was not prepared to go as far as his eager students, and their exaggerations of what they had heard from him, and their reports of chance phrases, were passed on bereft of both contexts and qualifications. They more than once imputed to him a weight of emphasis which he had not meant his words to carry, and committed him to positions by their excited talk which he would hardly have recognised. For he himself, in his *Introduction to Theology*, clearly stated that he undertook the work partly as an answer to those who trusted to human reason alone to establish the Faith on a sure and sound intellectual basis. He was writing to defend it from "those philosophers and heretics who vaunt themselves by opposing every creed by human rationalism, who pay no regard to any but such mundane arguments as they are acquainted with, and find many supporters from the fact that the majority of mankind are animal, but very few spiritual." In Abelard's mind a clear distinction existed between reason and rationalism, but it was a distinction which neither his enemies nor his pupils perceived, and for which he got no credit.

XXVII

The particular problem which Abelard most desired to make his own was that of the Holy Trinity. He had chosen to decorate the gateway of the Paraclete, which his scholars had built for him, with a sculptured representation of the Trinity, and it was to the honour of the Triune Godhead that he had at first thought of ascribing the new oratory. Thus, it was the first object of his scheme of theological inquiry to shed the light of reason upon the mystery of the Trinity, and to make the doctrine intelligible to the human intellect.

"The entire foundation of all that is good rests upon faith in the Holy Trinity." The more important, therefore, is it to provide an explanation "which is probable, agreeable to human reason," and which is capable of calling forth the allegiance of educated and thinking men. "The problem is to maintain together and at once the distinction between the three Persons, and their unity in the Godhead. This may best be done intelligibly by using some more homely and less ethereal analogy of some earthly substance and its inherent qualities."

He chose a brazen seal, and the passage in which he elaborated his analogy and its aptness is of great length and distinctly difficult. It amounts to this. A brazen seal is made of brass, with a pattern at the end, the impression of which is first taken upon wax, so that a distinctive pattern may be stamped upon letters and documents. Such a seal consists of matter and form; the matter being the brass of which it is made, the form being the distinctive impression it makes on wax, when used for stamping.

> Therefore, the brass itself, which is the matter of the brazen seal, and the seal itself of which that brass is the matter, are essentially one and the same thing. Yet the brass and the seal are so distinct in their properties, that the property of the brass is one, the property of the brazen seal another; and though they are essentially the same thing, yet the brazen seal is made of the brass, not the brass of the brazen seal. . . . Neither by any possibility can brass be its own matter, although it be the matter of the seal, from the very fact that it is brass. For brass is not made up of brass, as the seal is made of brass.

So far it is a case of two properties co-existing in one substance. But, for an analogy of the Trinity, a third property must be discovered in the brazen seal. Abelard affirmed that the third property was discernible as soon as, but not until, the seal had been used

for sealing. Then three properties appear within the
unity that is the piece of brass, the brass itself, its fitness
for sealing, and its act of sealing. " Since, then, its
essence is the same, whether as mere brass, as brass
which is capable of, or as brass which has been
employed for the act of sealing, which are three
distinct properties, these three properties are con-
joined one with another in such a manner that the seal
derives its power of sealing both from the brass and
from the brass which is capable of making an impression."

He then proceeded to point the moral and adorn
the tale.

> Just as the brazen seal is made of the brass, and in a
> certain way is born of it, so the Son has His being from
> the very substance of the Father, and is thus said to be
> born of Him. For . . . Divine Power is set forth by
> the name of the Father, just as Divine Wisdom is ex-
> pressed by that of the Son. But Divine Wisdom is, if I
> may so say, a certain power of God Himself, of such a
> kind as that by it He can guard Himself against all deceit
> and falsity, and through it can distinguish so correctly,
> and discriminate so acutely, that it is impossible that He
> should be mistaken or misled in anything.

That is the argument which is said to have incensed
his critics more than anything else he wrote. Some
called it Arianism, and others Sabellianism. But
while there was not general agreement on the exact
affinities of the heresy, there was a striking unanimity
among the theologians of the mystical school that it
was heretical.

The intricacies of the brazen seal by no means

exhausted his powers of analogy and exposition. He elaborated the germ of the idea he had expressed poetically in the last verse of *O Quanta Qualia*.

> Low before him with our praises we fall,
> Of whom, and in whom, and through whom are all;
> Of whom, the Father; and through whom, the Son;
> In whom, the Spirit, with these ever one.

"Of, Through, In"—the exact shade of difference could hardly be put more precisely than in the poetry of mysticism where he left it to the imagination of the reader. The same idea expressed in cold prose is no more illuminating to the intellect, and a good deal less inspiring to the heart. "The property of the Father is to be unengendered: of the Son to be engendered: of the Holy Spirit not to be engendered but to proceed from the union of the first two."

It was, however, when Abelard turned to Plato for light on the doctrine that he was most interesting. The Platonists had said that there was a threefold division among the elementary powers of the universe, the One, Noûs, the World Soul, and Abelard claimed that in so saying they had anticipated the doctrine of the Church, for plainly the One typified the Father, Noûs the Son, and the World Soul the Holy Ghost.

Again, he identified the Members of the Trinity with their attributes, which, while not heretical, was in effect a challenge to the prevalent mysticism, for the weakness of mysticism as it is expressed is, and has always been, the denial of attributes to divinity. In the universe the qualities most plainly discoverable are Power, Wisdom, Love: he identified these with

the Father, the Son, and the Holy Spirit respectively.
But he was careful to clear himself of the charge of
tritheism which this identification involves unless it is
qualified. "While these properties are distinct, all belong
to the nature of each." Divine Power presupposes
Wisdom and Love. Wisdom is both powerful and
loving, or it is not wisdom; the Love bereft of power
and Wisdom sinks into its own perversion, senti-
mentality. All this, he said, could be shown from the
Scriptures, but he turned mainly for his proofs not to
the Scriptures, nor to the Fathers, but to the philosophers. Thus one priest, Baronius, said of him,
"Peter Abelard has submitted the Scriptures to the
philosophers, chiefly to Aristotle, and he treats the
Fathers as ignorant folk who could prove nothing
that they said." Baronius distorted the facts, but he
spoke for many.

But though Abelard chiefly prided himself on the
light he had thrown on the mystery of the Trinity, it
was in his statement of the problem of the Atonement
that he worked his most profound and far-reaching
revolution.

> He died that we might be forgiven,
>   He died to make us good,
> That we might go at last to heaven,
>   Saved by His precious blood.

The children's hymn provides what is, perhaps, still the
best and the simplest statement of the Atonement, and
the problem is to explain how Christ's death had then
and has still that effect upon sinners.

For centuries what is called the Ransom Theory had

held the field; and although Anselm had shaken it in his *Cur Deus Homo*, it was left for Abelard finally to break it. His breaking of it was a deliverance of the Church from a desperately bad theological theory, but it was counted to him for iconoclasm rather than righteousness, and one of the chief quarrels Bernard had with him lay in the fact that he had denied that it was necessary to believe that Christ paid a ransom to the devil, and that God was party to the transaction.

For the Ransom theory of the Atonement started from the belief that men were so deeply involved in sin that they were the just portion of Satan. God could not deny Satan's bond, to which men by their sins had bound themselves, without involving Himself in an injustice towards Satan, and in thus outraging justice, denying Himself. But it was vital that men should be delivered, and that deliverance involved the compensation of the devil. Only by just compensation could they be freed: they could not justly be snatched out of the devil's hand by an arbitrary exercise of divine power. There was only one possible and adequate compensation, the wholly righteous man, the Sinless Redeemer, God's Own Son. Thus, as though by an arrangement with the devil, Christ was allowed to suffer crucifixion, being given over to death by the Father. Yet, in concluding this bargain, Satan over-reached himself. He could not hold his Victim, for the Victim was Himself Very God. Thus he was tricked, but most justly. Some writers, Augustine among them, had gone so far as to compare the Cross to a mouse-trap.

Such was the Ransom theory of the Atonement, and from it Abelard finally delivered the Church in his *Commentary upon St Paul's Epistle to the Romans*. He saw that any such theory inevitably postulated a God less than perfect, a loving Father involved in injustice towards His Son, and in sharp practice towards the devil. "Is it possible," he asked, "that the death of the Innocent Son has so pleased God that by it He has been reconciled to us, who have ourselves committed the sins which caused the innocent blood to flow?" How could the essential holiness of God, holiness far beyond any perfection that the mind can conceive, be anything but affronted by what was, on any showing, a travesty of justice? To assert it was to involve God in the absurdity of ethics by which He committed evil that good might follow it.

If, then, the Ransom theory was untenable, it remained to answer the question, How are we redeemed from our sins by the blood of Christ? The answer is the heart of the book, and the beginning of the new era in the history of the doctrine of the Atonement.

> The solution of this question appears to be that we are justified in the blood of Jesus Christ, and reconciled to God, in that by the unique grace which He has manifested to us in giving us His Son, who has taken our nature upon Himself, and persevered in it even unto death, in order to teach us in that way, by word and by example, He has attached us more firmly than ever to Himself by the power of His Love. Thus, true charity, enflamed by so great a benefit of divine grace, no longer recoils from any suffering borne for Him. And so by the power of the Passion men are made more righteous, that is more loving towards God. Our redemption therefore lies in the

supreme love of Christ for us, who, by His Passion, has
not only delivered us from the slavery of sin, but has
achieved on our behalf the glorious liberty of the children
of God, so that from that time forward all we did was
done from the love and not the fear of Him who won for
us a benefit so uniquely great that it is not possible that a
greater could be invented.

It is perhaps fitting that the greatest of all his poems,
Solus Ad Victimam Procedis, should celebrate the same
theme. It would be quite impossible to improve
upon Miss Helen Waddell's translation.

> Alone to sacrifice Thou goest, Lord,
>   Giving Thyself to death whom Thou hast slain.
> For us Thy wretched folk is any word,
>   Who know that for our sins this is Thy pain?
>
> For they are ours, O Lord, our deeds, our deeds,
>   Why must Thou suffer torture for our sin?
> Let our hearts suffer for Thy passion, Lord,
>   That sheer compassion may Thy mercy win.
>
> This is that night of tears, the three days' space,
>   Sorrow abiding of the eventide,
> Until the day break with the risen Christ,
>   And hearts that sorrowed shall be satisfied.
>
> So may our hearts have pity on Thee, Lord,
>   That they may sharers of Thy glory be:
> Heavy with weeping may the three days pass,
>   To win the laughter of Thine Easter Day.[1]

Nothing that Abelard wrote was comparable in
importance with his statement of the Atonement.
For the future it was the beginning of modern theology; and in his own time it was profoundly daring.
Not even Anselm had gone so far. For the first time
a theory of the Atonement had been suggested in

[1] Helen Waddell, *Mediæval Latin Lyrics*, p. 167. (Constable.)

which there was no taint or shadow of a vicarious
punishment due to men, but borne by Christ as a
sacrifice demanded by God to allay His outraged
justice. God was made love even in the Atonement,
even in the supreme act in which love seemed to
suffer defeat. And love is exalted to the supreme
good, and shown to be never so completely itself as in
sacrifice. "By the power of the Passion men are
made more righteous, that is more loving towards
God." His statement also made it clear that Christ's
power to save was not efficacious in death alone.
And, above all, it was not a legal fiction. It was
"practical": it "worked." "It really does make
men better instead of merely supplying the ground on
which they should be considered good, or excused
punishment for their sin, without being any better
than they were before." [1]

He also dealt at some length with such thorny
problems as Original Sin, and the damnation of
unbaptised babies. Here too the touchstone of truth
which he seeks to apply is the same, the utter necessity
that no statement of a doctrine should be made in
such terms as seem to impute to God what to the best
of men is immorality, which was itself the echo of a
platonic principle.

But not even Abelard was sufficiently advanced to
assert that the unbaptised escape the condemnation of
Hell. Yet they do, he said, escape the pains of Hell
in so far as they are physical. Their pain is spiritual,
and is caused by the loss of the vision of God. After

[1] Hastings Rashdall, *Doctrine and Development*, p. 137. (Methuen.)

his great statement of the doctrine of the Atonement, this is disappointingly halting and lame. Yet it was bold and original in his time. He felt it was impossible to go farther in the face of many of the Bible stories, for though he differentiated between the functions of the different parts of the Bible, he never dreamed of denying its complete and infallible inspiration. He makes his difficulty clear in the course of a statement on the question of original sin.

> Then, say you, they must be condemned who have not sinned, great iniquity; that they must be punished who have not deserved it, horrible atrocity. Yes, it is: *for men but not for God* (italics mine). The question is how to avoid accusing God of having drowned little children in the waters of the deluge, or burning them in the fire of Sodom. How could He allow the persecution and affliction of hapless Job and the martyred Saints? And could He allow the death of His only Son? You reply by an advantageous dispensation of His grace? Well and truly said.

The last quotation shows clearly enough that there were definite limits to the modernity of Abelard. Though in many respects he blazed the trail which subsequent generations were to follow, particularly in his exposition of the Atonement, his exaltation of reason, and his application of dialectical methods to the statement of theological problems, in many more he was the child of his own generation. He did not escape—who does escape it?—the most powerful of all educative forces, the conventions and mental habits of the society in which he lived. His scholarship, his boldness in exposition, and his originality, though they startled most men of his day, were still

—with the magnificent exception of his doctrine of the Atonement—not more than extensions of well-worn modes and conventions. Most of his characteristics were thoroughly mediæval. Of the seven deadly sins he sinned most deeply against the typically mediæval *Accidie* or Wanhope—the sin of gloom. There was in him more than a little of the mediæval puritan, despite his association with Heloise. No one decried louder than he the laxness of many of the monasteries of his time; and notwithstanding the fascination he unfailingly exercised over the minds of the young, he could still ask plaintively, "Why do not the Bishops and Doctors of the Christian religion expel from the City of God those poets whom Plato forbad to enter into his city of the world?"

He has often been called the first Protestant, and if to be a Protestant is to insist on the supremacy for human beings of human reason, and, by implication, on the duty of private judgment, the title is just. But if he heard the title, he would turn in his grave. There might certainly be the duty of private judgment, but for him it was utterly subordinate to the greater duty of being a faithful and obedient son of the Church. He never imagined that he was anything else but a good churchman, and to the end of his life he never believed that he had written or spoken one heretical word. There is not an iota of truth in the assertions of those who would claim him as the happy and heretical warrior rejoicing in open conflict with the Church of his time. The true Abelard speaks, on the contrary, in the preface to his *Introduction to Theology*.

I shall always be ready to give satisfaction for any error, correcting or effacing anything wrong that I may have said, when some faithful Christian, having convinced me by the light of reason or the authority of Scripture, so shall order me. . . . If it should happen that I am advancing any errors, I shall not defend them disdainfully, nor hold to them presumptuously. If I am not exempt from the faults of ignorance, at least I have done nothing to encourage an accusation of heresy, for it is not ignorance but obstinacy and blindness which make the heretic.

Thus, to be condemned for the hideous crime of heresy was for him the last and worst of evils, and it was a condemnation he had now to endure.

XXVIII

The *Historia Calamitatum* was written in 1135. It covers the events of Abelard's life up to that date. He had eight more years to live, but until the great and final drama was staged in Sens in 1140 we have no clear and continuous view of his movements and occupations. The curtain is only lifted fitfully and occasionally by stray references in contemporary documents.

On leaving St Gildas he had hidden himself in some unknown retreat, for he knew that the leaders of the monks he had dispossessed were looking for him. But that period cannot have lasted for much more than a year, for in 1136 he was teaching again in the school on the hill of St Geneviève in Paris. Among his pupils of that time was no less a scholar than John of Salisbury, perhaps the greatest classicist of the Middle Ages. He, whose failings were certainly not those of undue enthusiasm and exaggeration, wrote of the experience later in his *Metalogicus*, and spoke for the many thousands whom Abelard had taught.

> When, as a lad, I first went into Gaul for the cause of study, I addressed myself chiefly to the Peripatetic of Palais, who then presided upon Mount Saint Genovefa, an illustrious teacher and admired of all men. There at his feet I acquired the first rudiments of the dialectical art, and snatched according to the scant measure of my wits whatever passed his lips with entire greediness of mind. Then, when he had departed, all too hastily as it seemed to me, I joined myself unto Master Alberic.

It was, coming from such a source, a true compliment.

We do not know the cause of his sudden departure, but it took place in 1137. Probably it was due to a sudden and overwhelming bout of fear, for the storm clouds were fast gathering over his head. He conquered this attack, for in the next year he was again teaching in Paris, where he made the fatal friendship of Arnold of Brescia, a companionship which did him more harm than almost anything else. His past was coming home to roost, and whatever he now said or wrote was twisted into heresy. Whether he courted the position or not, he had become the centre of a strong movement for the freedom of human thought. Indiscreet disciples, such as Peter Berenger, who had not really understood his doctrines, went about the kingdom preaching rank heresy and saying that they were handing on the precepts of the great Master Peter Abelard. They varied it by wholesale abuse, both vulgar and ill-formed, of men such as St Bernard; and their errors of discretion and taste recoiled not upon their own heads but upon Abelard's. The strain made him querulous. He involved himself in a quite needless quarrel with St Bernard, and then, in a sermon preached upon St John the Baptist's day, went out of his way to denounce St Norbert, whom he accused of trafficking in false miracles, and of having faked a rising from the dead. Norbert's miracles were certainly rather startling, even for the Middle Ages, but he had died in 1134, and it was an error in tactics, to say the least, to provoke so needlessly the temper of his powerful enemies, which was already fully roused. A letter of Hugh Metel, Canon of St Léon of Toul, pupil of Anselm of Laon, written to Abelard, spoke for the more moderate of his foes.

> What presumption it is for a fallible mortal to wish to rise to the explanation of the Incomprehensible Trinity. Do you forget that only the ignorant can know God? Not that I desire to attack your learning and fame. That would be to wish to obscure the sun. You indeed possess prudence, eloquence, and the airs and graces of the mind, but there are perhaps some words you have thrown to the winds, which you have not fully understood. . . . Remember that you are a man, not an angel.

But it was reserved for William, Abbot of St Thierry, to loose the storm. St Thierry was a Benedictine abbey, but William was a Cistercian, who had been trained at Clairvaux by St Bernard, whose close friend he had remained. He was pleasantly engaged upon a Commentary on the *Song of Songs*, when someone rather maliciously brought him copies of Abelard's

theological works, and suggested that he might care
to read them. He did read them—with horror and
incredulity at such an indecent exhibition of human
reason. So appalled was he that he decided that something must be done at once. He immediately laid
aside his Commentary, and composed a lengthy and
remarkable letter, of which he sent copies both to
Bernard at Clairvaux, and to the Bishop of Chartres.

I am confounded before you, my lords and fathers,
when I, a person of no consideration, am compelled to
address you on a subject of great and general importance.
. . . For seeing, as I do, that Faith which is the hope of
us all, dangerously and grievously injured, no man gain-
saying or resisting—the Faith which Christ consecrated
by the shedding of His blood, for which Apostles and
Martyrs have fought even unto death, which holy
doctors, by their severe and manifold labours, have
transmitted to these wretched times sound, complete, and
incorrupt—I wither and pine away, and, for very anxiety
of heart and sorrow of spirit I am driven to speak in
defence of that for which, if it were necessary or fitting,
I would lay down my life. Nor is the danger concerning
minor points only, but threatens faith in the Blessed
Trinity, in the Person of the Mediator, in the Holy Spirit,
in the grace of God, in the mystery of our common
redemption.

Peter Abelard is again teaching novelties, again writing
about them. His books pass the seas, cross the Alps;
his new notions and dogmas about the Faith are carried
through kingdom and province; they are preached
before many, and as freely defended, in so much that they
are reported even to have influence at the Court of Rome.
I tell you it is with danger to the Church, no less than to
yourselves, that you keep silence. We seem to reckon
it a small matter that that Faith is corrupted for which we
have denied ourselves. Lest we should offend men, we
do not fear to offend God. I tell you this evil has grown,

and is growing, and if it be not stopped, it will become a
serpent for which a charmer will scarce be found. The
reason I speak thus you now shall hear. I lately fell
by accident upon one of the works of that person,
which bore the title *The Theology of Peter Abelard.* (It
consisted of the *Introductio ad Theologiam* and the *Theologica
Christiana* bound together.) I acknowledge that I was
struck, and felt a curiosity to read the book. There were
two treatises containing almost the same things, except
that the one embraced them a little more than the other.
I have marked those passages which move me to anger,
and have annexed my reasons for being incensed. You
must judge whether I have been in the right or not.
Being vehemently disconcerted by innovations of
expression in matters of faith, by new discoveries of
unheard of senses, and having no one near me to refer
to, I have chosen you before all others, whom I could call
to the defence of God's cause and that of the whole
Latin Church.

For that man fears and dreads you. Shut your eyes,
and whom will he care for? And if he can say what he
does say now, what will he not say when he fears and
dreads no one? Most of our great masters of ecclesiastical learning being dead, this domestic enemy, rushing
in upon the deserted commonwealth of the Church, has
assumed to himself a very singular office in Her, doing
in the Holy Scriptures what he was wont to do in dialectics, advertising his own discoveries, his annual crop of
novelties. He, forsooth, is a critic of the Faith, not a
disciple; a reformer, not a learner.

Here are the positions maintained in his work, which
I have thought fit to bring to your notice.

1. That he defines faith as being the estimation of things
   not seen.
2. That the names of Father, Son, and Holy Ghost,
   according to him, are improperly applied to God,
   and that this is a description of the fullness of
   the highest good.

3. That the Father is full power, the Son a certain power, and the Holy Spirit no power.

4. Of the Holy Spirit, that He is not of the substance of the Father and the Son, as the Son is of the Father.

5. That the Holy Spirit is the Soul of the World.

6. That by free will, without the help of grace, we can will and act rightly.

7. That Christ did not take flesh and suffer that He might deliver us from the subjection of Satan.

8. That Christ, God and man, is not the third Person in the Trinity.

9. That in the Sacrament of the altar, the form of the former substance remains in the air.

10. That diabolical suggestions are made to men through physic.

11. That from Adam we do not contract the fault of original sin, but its punishment.

12. That there is no sin except in consenting unto sin, and in the contempt of God.

13. That sin is not committed by concupiscence and delectation and ignorance, and what is thus committed is not sin but nature.

These few points collected from his works I judged expedient first to show you, in order to stimulate you, and to excuse myself lest I should appear excited without a reason. I shall amplify what I now send, caring little if I offend you in speech, if I do not in doctrine. God is my witness that I loved him; but in such a cause as this no one shall ever be either my friend or neighbour. Nor can this evil be rectified by a warning or reproof, he himself having made it so public.[1]

Most of the letter, of course, is sheer rhetoric, though none the less effective for that. But there are interesting points about it. Why did William select the Bishop of Chartres as the co-recipient with

---

[1] Translated by Cotter Morison, *Saint Bernard*, pp. 253–256.

Bernard of his outburst? "That man fears and dreads you." Certainly, and with reason, he feared Bernard. But the Bishop of Chartres was the same Geoffrey who had sought to protect him at the Council of Soissons. It is difficult to believe that Abelard went in any fear of him. Another interesting point is William's remark at the end, when he suddenly cries, "God is my witness that I loved him." Between two such minds there can have been little in common, little soil for friendship to grow in. It is one more testimony, all the more eloquent because of its source, of the extraordinary fascination Abelard exercised over all upon whom he chose to exert it.

But the most interesting part of the whole letter is undoubtedly the list of thirteen heretical propositions he charges Abelard with maintaining. They are astonishing charges. In three of them, 1, 5, and 12, it seems impossible to detect even the slightest suspicion of unorthodoxy. Others, again, are ridiculous charges which, one would have thought, a child of ten could not have accused Abelard of maintaining. Such are numbers 2, 3, 10, and 13. As for the others, with one exception, not even the most prejudiced prosecuting council could read them into Abelard's work. The only partially valid accusation in the whole thirteen counts is that he had taught "That from Adam we do not contract the fault of original sin but its punishment." Even that, put in a different way, would be perfectly orthodox.

Now one may possibly accuse William of stupidity, but certainly not of dishonesty. He accused Abelard of having said, for instance, "that the Father is full power, the Son a certain power, and the Holy Spirit no power," either because he flagrantly misunderstood what was in the book, or because it really was there. If it was really written there, then some enthusiastically copying student had thought fit to "improve on his copy." Abelard enjoyed a circulation for his works which many a modern novelist would envy. They were ardently copied not by monks but by students and young clerks employed for the purpose. William of St Thierry's thirteen heretical propositions prompt the interesting reflection that possibly he had received a copy written by someone who had made very free indeed with the text.

The two copies of the letter were sent away. The Bishop of Chartres merely acknowledged its receipt in a curt letter. He remembered too well the fiasco of Soissons, and how impotent a figure he had cut. Bernard received it during the Lent of 1139 when he was with his beloved novices in the Abbey of Clairvaux. He read it with interest, even with eagerness, for though he had been growing uneasy about Abelard's theology for some time, he had characteristically waited for someone else to ask him to intervene. He highly commended William for what he had done, and the enthusiasm of his faith, but said that the matter must wait until Easter was over. Lent was the season of prayer not of controversy.

XXIX

Whatever the merits or demerits of William of St Thierry's letter it achieved the purpose for which it was written with striking success. The storm clouds had long been gathering about Abelard's head. Only a slight touch was needed to burst them, and this touch William's letter supplied. He had loosed the storm, and ushered in the overture to the last phase of the drama. The period between Easter of 1139 and 2nd June of 1140, when the Council of Sens met, was one of great activity.

The whole energy of the campaign against Abelard was really concentrated in the hands of one man, Bernard of Clairvaux, but that one man was one of the most powerful that Europe has ever seen.

St Bernard, the greatest and the best of the Cistercians, was at this time forty-nine years of age. For many years past he had enjoyed a power and prestige in Europe which was hardly to be equalled again until the time of Napoleon. He towered head and shoulders above any other figure in the Church, and Bishops, Cardinals, and Popes alike who had any knotty problems to solve usually sought to lay them at his feet. He himself had been responsible for most of their appointments. An endless stream of letters flowed from his room at Clairvaux, which, in Mabillon's edition, fill three heavy and closely printed volumes. They were written to correspondents of all ranks in all corners of Europe, and the advice or commands which they enjoined were nearly always acted upon. His lightest word was law. Nor was it only over the clergy and the prelates that he exercised this tremendous authority. His word made and guided Popes. Kings and feudal noblemen who had oppressed the Church in their lands might, and often did, defy the Pope. More especially had they done so in the time of the Schism. But as soon as Bernard was called in, it was indeed seldom that they did not capitulate.

Thus he spent much of his life travelling hither and thither through Europe on the affairs of the Church, though his only ideal of earthly happiness was to remain with his monks amid the terribly severe mortifications of Clairvaux. But his was the name that struck terror into the Church's enemies, and his was a reputation for saintliness that even the most abandoned ruffian hesitated to defy. No diplomatic mission was complete unless Bernard led it: no crusade was considered to be thoroughly inaugurated unless Bernard preached it. And although his methods were the reverse of diplomatic, he nearly always won the day. He could write thus, for instance, to no less a potentate than the King of France, whose kingdom had been placed under an interdict by the Bishop of Paris: "From whom but from the devil can I say that this policy of yours proceeds? Whatsoever it may please you to do with your own realm, and crown, and soul, we, as sons of the Church, cannot hold our peace in the face of the insults and contempt with which our Mother is trodden underfoot." Then, just when the king was about to yield, Pope Honorius II made the Church ridiculous by suddenly raising the interdict. For once, he had not consulted Bernard, who immediately wrote to him, "We have seen it and speak it with sadness that the honour of the Church has received no slight wound in the time of Honorius."

The man who exercised this enormous authority was described by one of the novices of his abbey as "meagre and emaciated. His skin itself was of the finest texture, with a slight flush of red on his cheeks, seeing that all the natural heat of the frame had been drawn thither by constant meditation and the zeal of his holy compunction. His hair was yellow, inclining to white; his beard was auburn, sprinkled towards the end of his life with grey." [1] It was small wonder that his body was emaciated, for the heroisms of asceticism he had endured, going far beyond what was required even by the Cistercian rule, had been exceeded only by the hermits of the Egyptian desert in the early centuries of the Church's history. He found that this severity of self-mortification enabled him to see more clearly the vision of God, and he counted it but a small price to pay, for his whole being was turned towards God. He was one of those rare souls who have been able to forget self, and this produced in him a singleness of heart and a disinterestedness of purpose which were responsible for the extraordinary range and power of his influence.

[1] Geoffrey. Later Abbot of Clairvaux. Translated by G. G. Coulton, *Five Centuries of Religion*, vol. i, p. 287. (Cambridge University Press.)

But in spite of his unswerving singleness of aim and purpose, his character was far from simple. It was a skein of shot silk—interweaved with opposing traits, and yet achieving a unity. He was too great and too well-beloved to be merely a fanatic of the type of St Norbert, but, on occasion, he could be as ruthless and incapable of seeing reason as the veriest fanatic in history. Otto of Friesingen, himself a Cistercian and a contemporary, suggests credulity as the underlying cause of that side of his nature which was the relentless fanatic. "Because of his zeal for the Christian religion," wrote Otto, "he was something of a fanatic, and from his habitual meekness was credulous, so that from the first cause he detested those teachers who might put too much reliance on human reason and worldly wisdom, and from the second he was too ready to lend a favourable ear to any account, however much it told against those teachers." Being intensely mediæval, he was an extremist, whether his extremism showed itself in the ruthless persecution of a suspected heretic, or in the splendour of his utterly self-forgetful love of Christ and his Church.

In the history books he has been unlucky in that his most important and dramatic act was the breaking of Abelard, and on that occasion he showed himself at his worst. It is the task of this narrative to present him in this light; but though he thundered so ruthlessly, intrigued so shamelessly, and acted so unjustly where *Rhinoceros Indomitus* was concerned, there was all the time another Bernard, gentle, humble, and loving. Mr George Moore chooses to dismiss him in three contemptuous words. The Abominable Bernard! [1] But believing what he did, and being what he was, he could take no other course. Nothing is to be gained from blaming Bernard for being himself.

His chief characteristic was that he really did love men. By his love he attracted and held the love of the young—and especially the love of his own novices at Clairvaux. As he moved slowly through Europe, transacting the business of the Church, his mind was always straying longingly to the novices he had left at Clairvaux. All his protestations that fame was a burden to him, and that he left his abbey only with great reluctance, were certainly true. His happiest days were those on which he was approaching Clairvaux again after some long and tiresome journey. Then the peasants would flock to meet him "from their rocky Alps, shepherds and cowherds, and all manner of country folk, crying from afar to seek his blessing; then they crept back up the mountain gorges to their flocks, talking together and rejoicing that they had seen the man of God, and that his hand had been stretched over them in blessing." [2] It did not occur to them that their greetings had given him inestimable joy. His love flowed too over the traditional enemies of Christianity, the Jews, and he constantly and publicly protested against the terrible massacres of Jews which took place in connection with the Second Crusade. Even Luther praised him.

Yet he could with one breath protest against the

[1] In his Introductory Letter to C. K. Scott-Moncrieff's *Edition of the Letters*, p. 17.
[2] G. G. Coulton, *op cit.*, vol. i, p. 298.

Jewish massacres, and with the next say, "The Christian exults in the death of a pagan, because Christ is glorified." He could at one moment extol the crowning virtue of humility, and then turn to wither a dangerous rationalist with a blast of sheer invective which not even Timon of Athens could have surpassed. Then he could turn the kaleidoscope again and write a stream of not too gentle sarcasm upon the æstheticism of Cluny, or to poor William of St Thierry, who had tried to express in a letter how greatly he loved him. In his writings a typical mediæval crudeness alternated with an eloquent tenderness of irresistible charm. It is still difficult to read with dry eyes his sermon on the occasion of his brother Gerard's funeral. Then one turns the page and reads a perfectly grotesque and almost blasphemously materialistic homily on the conception of the Blessed Virgin.

But in spite of these contradictions which put out of court any swift generalisations about his character, such as the statement of one writer that he was the spiritual ancestor of the modern American fundamentalist, it is still true to say that there have been very few men in all history who knew as well as he what is the meaning of the Christian virtue of humility. From the beginning of his life until the end of it he was a holy and humble man of heart, and he maintained his humility intact in spite of the severe temptation of his power. It took the Middle Ages fully to appreciate what that means.

Bernard had now been aware of Abelard's activities for a number of years. William of Champeau had first spoken to him years ago about his young, impudent, and successful rival in the schools of Paris, when, as Bishop of Chalons, he had been a frequent visitor to Clairvaux. Since then Bernard had watched his career with growing uneasiness. He was certainly unorthodox, and his mind moved in unaccustomed channels. That, in Bernard's eyes, was quite sufficient. Such people were enemies of the Faith, and they ought to be crushed. Particularly was that the case when the offenders had Abelard's popularity and influence with the young. For by now his earlier pupils had risen to positions of eminence. A number of them were bishops, and a few had even become cardinals. He was the centre of a growing movement of revolt against everything that Bernard held most dear. The Council of Soissons had failed to silence him. Moreover, though a Religious, he had left his abbey, which, in Bernard's eyes, was a very grave sin. Again in the world, he was teaching his dangerous doctrine, and all he said was being widely and enthusiastically spread over Europe. It was clear to him that something ought to be done to silence this heretic, but, now as always, Bernard would not move unless he was definitely asked to do so.

Before this Abelard had given him just cause of offence, but he had let it pass. It was when Bernard had been to visit the Abbey of the Paraclete, and had found that the nuns were making an unauthorised revision of the Lord's Prayer by saying, "Give us this day our supersubstantial bread," according to St Matthew's version of the prayer in the Vulgate—

Panem nostrum supersubstantialem da nobis hodie. Bernard commented that it seemed rather unnecessary, and there left the matter. But Abelard heard of it, and wrote Bernard a long letter, which began mildly enough by justifying the practice of the abbey, but which soon forsook its tone of mildness and became a tempestuous tirade in denunciation of the liturgical innovations introduced by Cistercian abbeys. It was merely a personal affront, and so Bernard ignored it; but the incident cannot have disposed him to look any more favourably upon its author. Abelard, no doubt, wrote in this vein, because he could not endure that anyone should venture to criticise Heloise.

But whereas the criticism of the Cistercian liturgy was a purely personal matter, and so could be disregarded, the books which William of St Thierry had sent seemed to be a direct attack on the eternal and imperishable Christian Faith, once for all delivered to the saints, and which was the world's only shield between civilisation and chaos. Plainly, such doctrine could not be ignored. When, after the Easter of 1139, he began to read the books he could hardly contain his rage. He rose from his reading with a fixed and inexorable determination that Abelard must be finally crushed and silenced. He had preached crusades before this, but here was a cause no less urgent, and an enemy far more dangerous to Christendom than the Turk. He could use his power to no better purpose than that of ensuring Abelard's condemnation. For owing to the man's notoriety the evil was spreading, and spreading fast and far. There was no doubt

of it. Girding himself for battle, he took up his pen
and began to write.

> We have fallen upon evil days.   Masters we have with
> itching ears.   The scholars shun the truth and turn them
> to fables.   In France we have a monk without rule, a
> prelate without care, an abbot without discipline; Peter
> Abelard disputing with boys, conversing with women.
> He does not approach alone, as did Moses, towards the
> darkness in which God was, but advances attended by a
> crowd of his disciples.   In the streets and thoroughfares
> the Catholic Faith is discussed.   Men dispute over the
> childbearing of the Virgin, the sacrament of the altar,
> the incomprehensible mystery of the Trinity.[1]

This was a very mild specimen of the letters which
began to pour like a flood out of the abbey of Clairvaux
to abbots, bishops, and cardinals, and the entire
Roman Curia. They all bore the same refrain—
Delenda est Abelard. Bernard proved himself a superb
propagandist, because he had been so horrified by
Abelard's application of reason to the mysteries of the
Faith, that he truly believed every word he wrote.
His letters were studded with vituperative phrases,
and he did not pause to consider their strict accuracy.

> Scrutiniser of majesty and fabricator of heresy, he
> deems himself able by human reason to comprehend God
> altogether.
> When he speaks of the Trinity, he stinks of Arius:
> when of grace, he stinks of Pelagius: when of the Person
> of Christ, he stinks of Nestorius.

Sentences such as these were of the normal stuff of
mediæval controversy. But when Bernard went on
to call Abelard "a thorough hypocrite, having nothing

---

[1] Translated by Cotter Morison, *op cit.*, p. 308.

of the monk but the name and habit," and to declare
that "he was the enemy of the Cross, and had wished
to rend the seamless robe of the Lord," he was giving
vent not only to a fanaticism perfectly fantastic, but
also to the spite of personal enmity. He was behaving
like some base parody of himself, but to his own age
he was infallible, and once he had turned his energies
to crushing Abelard, it was morally certain that
Abelard would be crushed. When fanaticism is
combined with real saintliness—though the latter
quality had temporarily deserted him—there is no
power that can withstand it.

Abelard had many friends, and among them several
Cardinals, but he was too impulsive to choose his
friends with an eye to their protective powers, and
his chief friend and ally at that time was an added
weight in the scale against him.

He was Arnold of Brescia, the notorious anti-
clerical religious reformer, who had openly mocked
at the Donation of Constantine, and had made Brescia
too hot to hold him. He was an old pupil of Abelard's who had come into prominence during the
schism of Anacletus. His mind was a combination
of asceticism and dreaming energy. "Learned in
the Scriptures," John of Salisbury called him, and his
study had made him yearn for a renewal of poverty
and simplicity, and also for freedom, undefined but
real, for the world at large. To go to the schools at
Paris he left Brescia a commune politically inde-
pendent and economically strong. He arrived home
again to find something very like civil war between

the citizens and the Bishop, who was trying to repudiate the privileges of the commune and to revive the temporal power of the Church. He flung himself passionately into the fray, as the cool judgment of Bishop Otto of Friesingen describes in his contemporary history, "with absoluteness of conviction, with the vigour of a manly eloquence, with the prestige of an immaculate life, and the enchantment of a moral idealism, this detractor of Bishops and priests, this persecutor of monks, who praised only the laity, came to espouse the cause of the commune."

That trouble died down rather too quickly for Arnold's vehemence, for he had realised none of his ideals. So he immediately caused another riot, this time a somewhat more joyful one, by calling on the clergy to save their souls by surrendering all their property to the laity. The laity cheerfully agreed; the clergy, needless to say, did not. For this he was condemned by the Pope, and was ordered to leave Brescia.

Italy was closed to him, so he set out to join his master and friend Abelard, pausing by the way to compromise himself still further by negotiating with the Albigensian heretics. Thus Arnold, a heretic several times over, joined himself to Abelard, who by this association had made himself doubly obnoxious to the powerful obscurantists. Bernard persisted in regarding Arnold as Abelard's lieutenant, and affirmed that there was a coalition between them. "A Goliath," he wrote, "has appeared armed for the conflict, preceded by his squire, Arnold of Brescia.

Their scales are so closely united that a breath cannot penetrate them. The wasp of France has given a hissing to the wasp of Italy, and both have attacked our Lord and His Church." Of anything like a definite coalition there is no evidence. But it is undoubtedly true that Arnold's zeal stiffened Abelard, and made him finally determine to try conclusions with his enemies, and to prove to the ecclesiastical world, breathlessly engrossed by the struggle, that he was no heretic.

In this way passed the summer and winter of 1139. When the new year of 1140 came, the hectic literary activities of Bernard on the one hand, and the irresponsible propaganda of the Goliards and of Arnold on the other had made inevitable a public trial of strength between the two antagonists and the forces for which they stood. The only question remaining to be answered was where and when it might take place.

Bernard was doubtful of the advisability of having a council summoned for the express purpose of trying Abelard for heresy. He remembered the fiasco of Soissons, which had merely resulted in Abelard's increased popularity, and had signally failed to silence him. Then there was the undoubted power and magic of his eloquence to take into consideration. Moreover, it might possibly happen that even Bernard would not be able to prevail against his powerful allies unless he could so arrange matters that the trial of strength should take place on an occasion and in an atmosphere particularly suitable for his cause.

General Councils were rather dilatory bodies for that purpose.

Abelard, too, had now realised that it must come to a public disputation in some form or other, and he had read the lesson of Soissons no less clearly than Bernard. There he had been summoned in the rôle of a suspected heretic to appear before a council the composition of which made it certain that his case would be judged before it was heard and justice denied. Surely there were two morals to be drawn from the proceeding at Soissons, first, that suspected heretics must avoid œcumenical councils, and second, that they would be wise to challenge their accusers first rather than to wait for their accusers to challenge them. But if he was to avoid a council, he must act before Bernard had one convoked. Only so could he avoid having his case heard before a tribunal which would certainly condemn him. He must be the indignant innocent, clearing his name by challenging his accuser to prove his libels. He must not be the prisoner in the dock pleading for his good name and his freedom before a cold and sceptical judge and jury. He must take the initiative. To wait would only be to play into Bernard's hands. His only chance of victory was to attack boldly and at once.

Fortune favoured him with just the chance he needed. For it happened that the new King of France, Louis VII, combined a great aptitude for tyranny with a superstitious but compelling veneration for the relics of the saints. A great ceremony had been arranged to take place in the Cathedral of

Sens in the spring of 1140, when the treasured and
sacred relics of martyred saints, which the Cathedral
guarded, were to be unveiled for the adoration of the
people by a great company of bishops and clergy. It
was to be an occasion of immense solemnity, and the
King himself had promised to be present. Royalty
and the feudal nobility had more than once succoured
Abelard in his hour of need, and it seemed to him that
he could state his case before no better tribunal.
Besides, it was well known that Bernard and the Archbishop of Sens were not on the best of terms.

He wrote therefore to the Archbishop, asking that
when the Veneration of the Relics was over, the
assembled company should turn itself into a synod,
under the Archbishop's chairmanship, and that he
should be admitted and allowed to reply to his adversary, and to vindicate the orthodoxy of his faith.
The Archbishop was flattered, and agreed. He
invited Bernard to come and sustain his charges.
But Bernard refused, saying that Abelard's books
were pernicious enough to condemn themselves
without any help from him, and that the prosecution
should stand in need of no pleading other than a
recital of what he had written. And in any case it
was the business of the bishops and not of a monk
to deal with heretics and to defend the faith. The
fact that on his own argument he had been assuming
episcopal functions for many months past did not
apparently strike him as inconsistent. But he tempered his refusal to meet Abelard in open debate by
writing a circular letter to his friends among the

bishops exhorting them not to fail to attend the
ceremony at Sens, and to show themselves faithful
friends of Christ by condemning Abelard.

Abelard in the meantime received the Archbishop's
consent to his proposals, and he and Arnold published
far and wide the news that at last Bernard was to be
met in open debate, and the issue of the theological
duel would be to show whether or no it was God's
will that the exposition of the Faith was to be for
ever shackled by the ignorance of the obscurantists
in power. He sent to all his friends and disciples,
asking them to come to Sens on the appointed day,
and support him. Thus he made certain of the widest
publicity, and all Christendom awaited the event with
the deepest interest. In the face of this ample publicity
Bernard's friends thought that it would be very pre-
judicial to his cause if he was not present himself, for
everyone knew that by his recent actions he had provoked the conflict. They remonstrated with him,
urging that his absence would probably involve the
triumph of error. Then he reluctantly consented to
be present, and himself to undertake the defence of
the Catholic Faith.

XXX

The Synod met on Sunday, June 2nd, 1140. It was
within the Octave of Pentecost, for in the twelfth
century the feast of Trinity had not been instituted.
The city was predominantly ecclesiastical, and for
many weeks past its citizens had chiefly talked of the

Veneration and Exhibition of the Relics which was to take place with all due solemnity and pomp in the cathedral on the Sunday, and the less sacred but even more exciting scenes which were to take place on the following days.

Bernard's disciples had been busy preparing the ground, and telling the people of Sens of the abominable heresies of Abelard. They imputed to him "perfidious dogmatism" and called him "a necromancer and familiar of Satan." Thus it was into a thoroughly hostile city that Abelard and his disciples entered. This hostility was deepened by the contrast between the general manner in the streets of Abelard and Bernard. For though Abelard was a sick and a tired man, and a suspected heretic, he was tall and still handsome, and he held himself erect as he walked. Pride and not shame was in his bearing. But Bernard lived up to his immense reputation for meekness and saintliness. Though he had consented unwillingly to come to Sens to uphold his cause, he declined to prepare any statement. "Take no thought how or what ye shall speak: for it shall be given you in that same hour what ye shall speak." That was the text on his lips. He rode into Sens alone, and the people crowded the streets to see him pass, and marked his emaciated condition, his lowered head, his rough Cistercian dress. His manifest humility proclaimed that he was the saint of God, and how then could they doubt that his was the cause of right? The people kneeled to receive his blessing as he rode by, and he exhorted them to pray for Abelard. Then, when he had passed, they stood up again and stared after him, telling each other the stories of his wonderful miracles.

On the Sunday, in the presence of the king, nobles, and clergy, and a vast congregation of the people the Veneration of the sacred Relics took place. The gorgeous vestments of the clergy and the gaily coloured clothes of the laity, set against the quiet grey-stone background of the cathedral, made it all an imposing and wonderful scene. As chant and the smoke of the incense rose and mingled impalpably, the shabbily clad Abbot of Clairvaux moved slowly hither and thither through the vast crowd, showing and explaining the relics to the king.

On the next day the members of the Synod met in the church of St Etienne to deal with the books of Abelard. There were present the king, Thibaud, Count Palatine, to whom the Church owed many pious foundations, William, Count of Nevers, who was soon to show the depth of his piety by becoming a Carthusian monk, and many other nobles. Henry, Archbishop of Sens, presided. He had brought with him all the bishops of his province, except those of Paris and Nevers. Geoffrey of Chartres was among them. By the Archbishop's side sat the Archbishop of Rheims, and, with him, three bishops of his province, among them Jocelyn, Abelard's old enemy, now Bishop of Soissons. Around the church were seated a mass of abbots, priors, archdeacons, and masters of schools, by far the greater part of them being Bernard's partisans.

The church was completely filled with this silent

and expectant company, when at last Abelard appeared
at the west door. The crowd opened to let him pass
up the nave. As he walked he looked about him and
saw Guibert de la Porée standing near, and he paused
to whisper a prophecy into his ears that he would be
the next to stand in his shoes, as indeed he was.
Bernard, clad in the white robe of a Cistercian abbot,
stood in the pulpit facing him, and holding in his hands
the incriminating books. From these books Bernard
had chosen seventeen heretical propositions, and in a
loud voice he now ordered them to be read out. As
the reading began Abelard stood listening in a bewil-
dered way, and looking round about him at the faces
of those who were sitting watching him. Suddenly,
before the recital of his heresies was ended, he cried
out that he would hear no more, but would appeal to
the Pope for justice, and, turning, rushed out of the
church.

The scene had been short but memorable, and the
monastic historians naturally attributed Abelard's
sudden flight to the intervention of God, who had
thus dramatically endorsed the action of His saintly
Abbot. He had been miraculously stricken, they said.
The suddenness of it all, and the consideration that
Abelard had himself asked for the Synod gave plenty
of credence to their view. But what had really
happened? Had his nerves suddenly failed again?
It might well be so, for his nerves had never been strong
to face inimical action, and his sudden uncontrollable
impulses had played him false before now. Moreover, he was ill and weary of the storms which had

for so many years been beating about his head, and he was now near his death.

Or did he depart so suddenly because he saw as in a flash that if he stayed his condemnation was a certainty, and that the tragic humiliation of Soissons was bound to be acted over again? It was probably a combination of the two impulses which drove him to his sudden decision, but as soon as he entered the church and saw the composition of the Synod, he must have known that his case was hopeless unless he could transfer it to some other court. For the atmosphere of the crowded streets, filled with citizens whose emotions had been stirred to militant and aggressive belief by the events of the previous day, and to whom he could only appeal through the intellect, was no more unfriendly than the atmosphere inside the church of St Etienne. As he looked round at the assembled prelates, he saw none who would be likely to espouse his cause in the very presence of Bernard. There was, it was true, Geoffrey, Bishop of Chartres, but of what avail had he proved at Soissons, when not Bernard but the far less powerful Alberic of Rheims had been the chief enemy? As for the others, the Archbishop of Sens had already been once deprived of his see by the Pope, and Bernard could easily have him deprived again. The Archbishop of Rheims was Bernard's nominee. The Bishop of Soissons was an old enemy. The Bishop of Arras had been the pupil, and novice, and still was the intimate friend of Gosvin, another determined enemy. And so with the others —there was not one on whom he could rely for any effective help. Moreover, he had asked for and expected a disputation not a trial. The fact that Bernard opened the case in the rôle of counsel for the prosecution showed that his plans had miscarried, that his dream was shattered. He would not face again the humiliation of Soissons, and so he went away to appeal to Rome.

Whatever his motive may have been, he had taken the only wise course left. For the Roman Court had been growing very jealous of the power and independence of the Church in Northern France, and might be very likely to welcome the chance of asserting its inherent superiority over any local Synod, however powerful its composition. It did not in fact happen, but there was a very good chance that it might, and, a few years later, the Pope did repudiate his dependence upon and his connection with Bernard. But that came too late to be of any service to Abelard.

When he had rushed out of the church so suddenly, there was a silence of blank astonishment, and when the members of the Synod recovered the use of their tongues, a confused debate as to what had better be done next followed. But it was soon ended by the summary authority of Bernard, who decided to judge Abelard's doctrine in his absence, since, as he said, the heretical propositions were all taken from his books, which had not been disavowed, and were those which had been notoriously and widely taught. "For the sake of the spirits they have already begun to corrupt it is essential that they shall be crushed."

The Archbishop of Sens, needless to say, made no objection, and the reading of the seventeen propositions began again. Many of the bishops, but above all Bernard, quoted freely from the Fathers, and especially from St Augustine, to prove by incontestable authority that they were heretical, and, from that vast storehouse of arguments, had no difficulty in finding plenty of evidence, for they ignored that which pointed the other way. But all that was only a matter of form, done in order to lend the appearance of justice and equity to proceedings in which justice was parodied. The propositions were all condemned, root and branch, and pronounced "pernicious, manifestly damnable, opposed to the Faith, contrary to truth, openly heretical."

The Synod did not itself pronounce any sentence upon Abelard. It merely condemned his teaching and that of his follower Arnold of Brescia. This mildness was not due to any unwontedly merciful mood; but Abelard had appealed to Rome, and therefore sentence must be left to the Pope. But the list of his heresies, which the Synod had condemned, was swiftly compiled and despatched to Rome. There were fourteen of them, of which only two need be mentioned here. Neither of them figures on William of St Thierry's list. His identification of the Persons of the Trinity with the attributes of Power, Wisdom, and Love was pronounced heretical in matter and in form, and as savouring of Arianism. Then his exposition of the doctrine of the Atonement was also condemned. To this list Bernard added a personal letter to the Pope, explaining his own position in the matter, and elaborating the errors set down in the official proceedings of the Synod. Its general trend shows how inconceivable it was to him that the methods of Abelard could ever result in anything but a studied insult to Christ and His Church. A faith explained was a faith destroyed.

Is it not wonderful if a man who cares not what his words may mean should rush in upon the hidden things of faith, and thus profanely invade and despoil the concealed treasures of devotion, seeing that he has no feeling either of piety or of allegiance to the Faith. At the very beginning of his *Theology*—or rather *Fool*-ology—he defines faith as being opinion. As if anyone might think or say what pleased him concerning it; or as if the sacraments of our faith, instead of reposing on certain truth, depended without certitude on wandering and various opinions, and rested not upon most undoubted truth. If the Faith is unstable, is not our hope in vain? Therefore the martyrs were foolish to endure such torments for an uncertainty; for the sake of a doubtful reward to pass through a painful death into everlasting exile. But God forbid that we should think as he does, that there is anything in our faith and hope which hangs upon a doubtful opinion. Rather let us hold that the whole is grounded upon certain, solid truth, preached divinely by oracles and miracles, established and consecrated by the childbirth of the Virgin, by the blood of the Redeemer, by the glory of the Resurrection. These testimonies have been made too credible for us to doubt them; and if they fail in any way, "the Spirit beareth witness with our spirit that we are the children of God."

How then can anyone dare to call faith opinion, except it be one who hath not yet received that Spirit, or ignores or disbelieves the Gospel? These ideas and opinions belong to the academics, who doubt of all things and know nothing. Therefore I walk safely, following the Apostle of the Gentiles; and I know that I shall not be confounded. . . .

His definition of faith, I confess, pleases me: "Faith is the substance of things hoped for, the evidence of things not seen." *The substance of things hoped for*, he says, not the fantasies of empty conjectures. You hear, *the substance*! You may not think or dispute on the Faith as you please; you may not wander here and there through the wastes of opinion, the by-ways of error. By the name *substance* something certain and fixed is placed before you; you are enclosed within certain boundaries, you are restrained within unchanging limits. For faith is not an opinion but a certitude.[1]

Abelard had left Sens on the day on which the Synod had come to its decision. He never reached Rome, and even if he had, it would have been a useless journey. For in spite of the influence of those cardinals of the Roman Court who had been friends and pupils of his, the confirmation of the order of condemnation was quickly sent. Bernard had asked that the Pope might "answer their unanimous prayer by confirming their sentence, and strike with a just chastisement those who in their obstinacy of contention continued to defend them (Abelard's errors), and, as became the successor of Peter, impose silence upon him from teaching and writing alike, and order the books to be suppressed." Promptly the answer came. "By these presents we command you to cause Peter Abelard and Arnold of Brescia, perverse manufacturers of dogma, impugners of the Catholic Faith, to be imprisoned separately in houses of religion wherever it may seem good to you, and to cause their books to be burnt

[1] Translated by Cotter Morison, *op. cit.*, pp. 317, 318.

wherever they may be found. Given at the Lateran.
18. Cal. August 1140."

Abelard was not destined to live again in the outside world. But for Arnold there was reserved a more
bitter end, when he would be hanged in Rome, his
body burned, and the ashes flung into the Tiber, that
no trace might remain of his seditious person. But
that time was not yet. When the official condemnation arrived from Rome, he was in Paris. Bernard had
him expelled thence, and then hounded him like the
Wandering Jew from one city in Europe to another.
From Paris he chased him to Zurich, and from Zurich
into Bohemia. He had only to write once to the
municipal authority of this "Arnold of Brescia, whose
conversation is honey, and whose doctrine poison,
who has the head of a dove and the tail of a scorpion
whom Brescia has vomited, Rome held in horror,
Germany abominated, and Italy will not receive," and
immediately the authority took steps, and Arnold was
chased away. To earn the disinterested enmity of
Bernard of Clairvaux was no light matter. The whole
force of it was now directed upon Arnold. For he
had done what Abelard had never done. He had
directly attacked the temporal power and property
of the Church, and thrown in his lot with undoubted
heretical sects. For seven years he was forced to
wander about Europe until in 1146 he at last went
back to Rome to begin the nine years' adventure,
which ended in his martyrdom.

XXXI

On the day that the Council published its decisions
Abelard left Sens for Rome. There, he was convinced, he would find the justice he had been denied,
for there alone could he hope to find a tribunal not
under the absolute domination of Bernard. Weak in
physical health, and prematurely aged by the storms of
his life, he travelled leisurely, staying several days at
each of the monasteries he passed on the way.

There were two things which he must do without
delay, and which could not wait until the Roman
Court had reached a decision, for that might very well
take months. Heloise must be reassured that her
husband, and now the mentor of her abbey, had been
wrongfully accused of heresy. First, therefore, he
wrote to her.

> Heloise, my sister, once so dear in the flesh, and to-day
> dearer still in Jesus Christ: Logic has made me hateful
> to the world. They say—they, to whom all knowledge
> is perdition—that while I am eminent in logic I have
> grievously failed in the knowledge of the science of St
> Paul. . . . It is, I think, fear rather than wisdom which
> judges me thus. I do not want to be a philosopher if
> the price of it is that I must rebel against St Paul; I have
> no desire to be even Aristotle if I am thus to be separated
> from Christ. For there is no other name under Heaven
> in which I can find any hope of Salvation. For Christ,
> who reigns at the right hand of the Father, I love and
> worship.

He then wrote a confession of his faith. It was a

simplification of what he had already said, and, in this form, the most pertinacious examination can find no heresy. "That is the faith in which I find repose. That it is which gives me strength and hope. Fortified by this assurance of safety I do not believe in the abomination of Scylla, and I laugh at the gulf of Charybdis, nor do I fear the compelling songs of the Sirens. Let the tempests come and the winds blow in their fury, I shall not be shaken, for I am founded upon an unconquerable rock."

When this letter had been written he began the heavier task of composing a long *apologia*, written temperately and dispassionately, defending himself against the attacks made upon him, and elaborating the confession of faith he had already sent to Heloise. He did not, however, finish it until he was at Cluny, and then he addressed it to "the Children of the Christian Church." There is no known copy of this work, but a few sentences from the beginning of it were quoted by Otto of Friesingen in his contemporary history.

In the meantime another apologist had, without being invited, hurled himself into the fray on Abelard's behalf. His utter lack of any sense of proportion, his total inability to understand any other point of view than his own, made his contribution to the controversy so cheerfully libellous that it adds a welcome note of comedy to the tragic story, but is an excellent example of how greatly Abelard suffered from the well-meaning efforts of his friends. Peter Berenger, who came from Poitiers, and had been one

of Abelard's pupils, sat down after the Synod of Sens
was over and composed an *Apology for Abelard*, which
he sent to Bernard. So great is his wrath that he
cannot maintain the note of elaborate mock humility
with which he begins, but soon asks crudely, "was it
not painful to you to meet with anyone who could
answer you with impudence equal to your own?"
Then he accuses Bernard of vomiting over Abelard
the poison of his wrath, of rushing at him like a
murderer in an ambush, of hypocrisy, in that "you
harangued the people, bidding them pray to God for
him, while in private you took means to get him
prescribed." There follows a very graphic but completely libellous account of the proceedings of the
Synod, in which he says that all the Bishops were
drunk, so drunk that they could not even say *Dam-
namus* properly as the condemned propositions were
read out, but could achieve only the end of the word
—*namus*, and then, tired out by this effort, relaxed
once more into drunken slumber. Finally, his honest
indignation overcomes all other emotions. He ceases
from trying to be ironic, and roundly bids Bernard
remember that Abelard is "just as much a Christian
as you are. And, if you wish, he will be a Catholic,
just as you are. Or, if you do not wish it, he will
be a Catholic none the less: for God belongs to
us all, and is not the private property of any one
person."

From the other side came a work equally violent
and equally absurd, written by some unknown Abbot,
who dedicated it to the Archbishop of Rouen. He

accused Abelard of being incited by mad devils to destroy the Church, and of having spoken of Bernard as Satan, the father of all devils, masquerading as an angel of light.

But Bernard was too great a man to be deflected from his course by mere abuse or to be incited to it by bitterness, and Abelard had suffered too deeply to care very much. He went on his way to Rome, passing through Burgundy on the road to Lyons. He came to Cluny late one evening, and there asked for hospitality, which the Abbot, Peter the Venerable, at once gave him, treating him more as an honoured guest than a dishonoured heretic.

Cluny, not far from Mâcon, was the most famous abbey in Europe. The magnificence of its church, the lavishness of its hospitality, the treasures in its library had provoked the disapproval of Bernard, but drew pilgrims from far and wide. Its Abbot, by virtue of his office, inherited a priority in station over the other Abbots of Europe, and that priority was amply maintained by Peter the Venerable, whose sheer goodness of heart had won for him a prestige only surpassed by that of Bernard.

He gave Abelard a warm welcome, and pressed him to stay for several days, for he saw in him not so much a condemned heretic—and his hatred of heresy was not less than that of Bernard—as a weary and unhappy man, whose world had crumbled about his feet. He asked him about his plans, and when he told him, he praised "his design and advised him to seek a refuge known and open to all." But as the days passed, and as he enjoyed the welcoming peace and love to which he was sadly unaccustomed, the project of appealing to Rome seemed less urgent and immediate. Peter perceived what was passing in his mind, and suggested that it might be better to seek a reconciliation with Bernard. Abelard warmly welcomed the suggestion. He was ill, and weary of strife and journeys, and Peter had suggested too that he might very well stay at Cluny, and assume once more the monastic life. At Peter's invitation, therefore, the Abbot of Citeaux came to Cluny to consult with them, and act as a mediator between him and Bernard. We do not know the details of the negotiation which followed, but his new "Apology" was taken to Bernard, very likely by the Abbot of Citeaux, and with the confession of faith therein contained he declared himself satisfied. Then it was arranged that the bitterness between the two should be finally washed away by a meeting. It took place, and Abelard returned to Cluny joyfully announcing that all the old animosities had now been removed in peace.

His long persecution was over, and now he only wanted a refuge. He gladly agreed to remain at Cluny at the side of the peacemaker, Peter. Permission from Rome, since Peter himself asked it, was easily forthcoming, and Abelard settled down to spend the evening of his days amid the peace, the love, and the beauty of Cluny. He was made the Head of the Congregation, and, as Abbot, held an honoured place in the abbey second only to Peter himself.

It was an honour, but to Abelard as he now was

it was irrelevant. For a curious change had been wrought in him, a change of which his eagerness to be reconciled to Bernard had been a symptom. What the bitter discipline of persecution had failed to achieve had been brought about by the love and compassion shown by Peter the Venerable. Pride had been born in him by his great achievement in ousting William of Champeau from the schools, and since that time it had dogged his footsteps like a misbegotten shadow. Now he had put away pride, and, deprived of it, had found the joy of humility. That humility had to be expressed within the set monastic and ascetic channels, but it was none the less real and joyful. The change in his character and his bearing was the amazement of the Cluniac monks. "Not even St Germain," said Peter, "showed a more abject spirit, nor St Martin a greater love of poverty." He threw himself whole-heartedly into the uttermost austerity of the Benedictine Rule, walking wrapt in meditation, with lowered head, regarding himself not as a man famous throughout Christendom, but as less worthy than even the novices in the abbey. He divided his time between frequent attendance at the services, reading, and prayer; but always he was silent. His submission had come late, but when it came it was the more complete.

He fell ill of a most painful disease of the skin, and as he did not recover from it, Peter thought that a change of air might relieve him. So he sent him to the daughter-house of Cluny, the Priory of Chalons, in a district which was famed for the strength of its air. There he lingered for a little, reading as long as he was able, and then praying incessantly. But the disease took a fatal turn. He knew that the time of his death had come, and, having confessed his sins, recited the articles of his Christian Faith, and having received, in the presence of all the monks, the Blessed Sacrament, he died.

XXXII

Some years before, he had asked that when he was dead his body might be taken to his Abbey of the Paraclete, and there given to Heloise for burial. Peter the Venerable knew of this wish and determined to carry it out. But before that could be done the bitter news had to be broken to Heloise. Peter wrote her a letter of great tenderness and beauty, speaking of the manner of her husband's life at Cluny, showing that his end was not without its note of triumph:

Thus Master Peter brought his days to their end: and he who for his supreme mastery of learning was known wellnigh over the whole world and in all places famous, continuing in the discipleship of Him who said "Learn of me, for I am meek and lowly in heart," so to Him passed over as I must believe. Him therefore, O sister most dear, him to whom you once clung in the union of the flesh and now in that stronger finer bond of the divine affection, with whom and under whom you have long served the Lord, him, I say, in your place or as another you, hath Christ taken to His breast to comfort him, and there shall keep him, till at the coming of the Lord, the voice of the archangel and the trump of God descending, He shall restore him to your heart again.[1]

[1] Translated by Helen Waddell, *The Wandering Scholars*, p. 109.

Peter himself took the body to the Abbey of the Paraclete, and gave Heloise what comfort he could. She thanked him with an austere simplicity. "You have given us the body of our master," and could say no more. He stayed at the abbey for several days, and preached to the nuns. Then, when he left, she asked him for one more favour, that he should formally absolve her husband from his sins. It had to be done in writing as well as by word of his mouth, for it was a custom in the twelfth century to hang over the gravestone of the departed spirit the parchment on which the absolution was written. Immediately Peter had returned to Cluny he confirmed in writing the absolution he had pronounced, and Heloise, who had buried the body of her husband in the precincts of the abbey he had founded and given to her, hung over his tombstone, engraved with an elaborate epitaph, a parchment, sealed with Peter's ring, on which there was written: "I, Peter, Abbot of Cluny, who received Peter Abelard into the monastery of Cluny, and gave his body into the keeping of the Abbess Heloise, and the Religious of the Paraclete: by the authority of Almighty God and of all the Saints, and according to my office, I absolve him from all his sins."

XXXIII

His had been a stormy, turbulent life, lived in alternating extremes of sorrow and joy, despair and triumph, hatred and popularity. Like many other men, of whom it may be said that history was different because they lived, in his life he saw only the ruin of every cause for which he had fought. Yet, though he could not know it, and though nobody could then foresee it, he was everywhere triumphant. The famous victory of St Bernard seemed to be final, and yet it was the high-water mark of the falling tide of the older mediæval thought. After the Synod of Sens it steadily ebbed.

At the Council of Soissons he had been condemned in part for his unheard-of audacity in suggesting that classical and theological learning went well together. Yet in the next generation there arose the greatest classical scholar of the Middle Ages, the Englishman, John of Salisbury, who was regarded as no less orthodox on account of his scholarship, who was present at the martyrdom of St Thomas of Canterbury, and who held the famous bishopric of Chartres when he died. In the *Sic et Non* Abelard had, in a most devastating manner, brought the principles of dialectics to bear upon the interpretation of the Scriptures. It filled all good Churchmen with horror. Yet such was precisely the method adopted in the next generation by Peter Lombard in his *Sentences*, the theological textbook on which all the Schoolmen, including that supreme buttress of orthodox Catholicism, Thomas Aquinas, were brought up. Bernard had broken him, as he said over and over again, because of his presumption in claiming that reason could be an interpreter and an ally of the Faith. Yet Aquinas and Duns Scotus hardly wrote a line without invoking the aid of reason. The Synod of Sens had condemned before all else his repudiation of the Ransom theory of the Atonement. Yet the Ransom theory abruptly disappeared from Catholic theology.

Abelard had won all along the line. It is significant that when, not many years after his death, Bernard had his successor, Guibert de la Porée, prosecuted for much the same offences, the prosecution ludicrously failed. Abelard affords an example of the common saying, an example more apt and complete than history usually provides, that the heresy of one generation is the orthodoxy of the next.

In everything he was creative. His love for Heloise, and her unending and unconquerable devotion to him, provide history with one of its greatest stories, and literature with some of its greatest letters. That love was an event which dominated all his life, and nothing that he did is wholly explicable as apart from it. No historian can ignore it.

But he left the world more than a story. He was the direct intellectual ancestor of the Schoolmen, whose influence upon history is not even now exhausted. But whether in the future any large body of educated people will continue indefinitely to turn to Aquinas for their theological justification and method is open to doubt. Even now his influence is waning.

But there is one gift of Abelard's which has gone from strength to strength, and is to-day everywhere growing in power and prestige. That gift is the university. Doubtless the university system of education would have been evolved even if he had never been born, for it is rather true that the general love of learning made him what he was than that he made the general love of learning. But there is no doubt that he, more than any other man, speeded the process and conditioned the form. Universities were founded upon the necessity of safeguarding privileges and maintaining order. While schools were small there was no need of elaborate machinery for these purposes. It was his name, and the magic of his eloquence, which drew so many scholars to Paris that the authorities were forced to elaborate machinery for controlling them. It was his teaching, and the challenge of his intellectual power, which helped to spread in increasingly wide circles all over Europe the burning ambition to be learned.

The new era of the Golden Middle Age, of which he was the herald, was built upon and conditioned by the new educational instrument of the university, and of all the gifts which he gave none was more vital for history than this.

XXXIV

Abelard died on 21st April 1142, and Heloise ate out her heart for another twenty-two years before her spirit was set free to join his. Her body was laid to rest in the crypt of the Abbey of the Paraclete, wherein her husband's body lay, but it was not buried in the same tomb. So they lay for six hundred and fifty years, until at last, by order of the Government of the day, their remains were carried to the famous cemetery of Père Lachaise in Paris. There their dust was mingled, and buried under a stone plinth, bearing the words ABELARD: HELOISE—For Ever One. And there, to this day, they lie together.

INDEX OF NAMES AND PLACES

Wandering Scholars   Helen Waddell
medieval Latin Lyrics   "   "

nominalism: no reality to universal concept
realism: (Platonic) universals like genus + species
        have sep. existence apart fr. individuals that are
        tributary to them

Anselm = teacher + patron of realist Wm of Champeaux
        Abelard (nominalist) condemns Wm.

novel by Geo. Moore